# Drupal 6 Site Blueprints

Ready-made plans for 12 different professional
Drupal sites

**Timi Ogunjobi**

BIRMINGHAM - MUMBAI

# Drupal 6 Site Blueprints

First published: August 2009

Production Reference: 2140809

Published by Packt Publishing Ltd.
32 Lincoln Road
Olton
Birmingham, B27 6PA, UK.

ISBN 978-1-847199-04-1

www.packtpub.com

Cover Image by Karl Moore (karl.moore@ukonline.co.uk)

# Credits

**Author**
Timi Ogunjobi

**Reviewers**
Dan Morrison

Ken Rickard

**Acquisition Editor**
David Barnes

**Development Editor**
Dhiraj Chandiramani

**Technical Editor**
Hithesh Uchil

**Copy Editor**
Leonard D'Silva

**Editorial Team Leader**
Akshara Aware

**Project Team Leader**
Priya Mukherji

**Project Coordinator**
Ashwin Shetty

**Proofreader**
Dirk Manuel

**Indexer**
Monica Ajmera

**Production Coordinator**
Dolly Dasilva

**Cover Work**
Dolly Dasilva

# About the Author

**Timi Ogunjobi** is a Technical Writer, Web Developer, and Open Source evangelist. Trained as an engineer, Timi has been developing web applications, in several frameworks, for more than five years, and has also been writing, for more than a decade, on a wide variety of topics, including fiction, business, and technology.

Timi balances his time between programming, reviewing, writing, and contributing to interesting web-based and community projects. When he isn't working (which isn't that often) he enjoys playing jazz guitar and getting involved in outdoor activities—principally cricket, golf, and swimming.

Timi is the principal architect of Websesame—www.websesame.com—a software development and technical writing company based primarily in London, but also with a presence in USA, and in Africa to where he loves to retreat. Websesame typically undertakes CMS, LMS, and ERP based projects and web applications in particular.

Timi has previously had another Drupal book published, titled "Adventures in Drupal". He has also published several fiction and nonfiction books, and has been featured in several anthologies.

The creation of this book was first made possible by God.

Then it was made possible by David Barnes of Packt Publishing who said "If you think it is possible, then go for it!".

My family facilitated the creation of this book by knowing how important it is to keep out of my way (especially when I am on a mission from God).

Finally, it was made possible by me, of course.

I thank you all for reading ... and also give special thanks to Lyn Brown.

# About the Reviewers

**Dan Morrison** is `dman` on `Drupal.org`. He has been working with computers since the times when 3.5 KB RAM was a big deal, the Internet since the days it was in black and white, and text-only, and has been developing almost exclusively with Drupal for several years now.

Based in Wellington, New Zealand, he helped develop New Zealand's first online banking system in 1997. Since then—in between periods spent juggling cocktails in disco bars—he's worked on many different web sites, including several of the largest intranets in New Zealand.

Currently he spends too much time making things in Drupal just because they are cool, and works at helping companies and government departments with semantic data migration and metadata publishing in his spare time. Late at night, he helps on the Drupal forum and struggles with source control.

He likes coffee, cats, and cocktails.

**Ken Rickard** is a senior programmer at `Palantir.net`, a Chicago-based firm specializing in developing Drupal web sites. He is a frequent contributor to the Drupal project and is the maintainer of the Domain Access, MySite, and Menu Node API modules. At Palantir, he architects and builds large-scale web sites for a diverse range of customers, including Foreign Affairs magazine and the University of Chicago.

From 1998 through 2008, Ken worked in the newspaper industry, beginning his career managing web sites, and later becoming a researcher and consultant for Morris DigitalWorks. At Morris, Ken helped launch `BlufftonToday.com`, the first newspaper web site launched on the Drupal platform. He later led the Drupal development team for `SavannahNOW.com`. He co-founded the Newspapers on Drupal group (`http://groups.drupal.org/newspapers-on-drupal`) and is a frequent advisor to the newspaper and publishing industries.

In 2008, Ken helped start the Knight Drupal Initiative, an open grant process for Drupal development, funded by the John L. and James S. Knight Foundation. He is also a member of the advisory board of PBS Engage, a Knight Foundation project to bring social media to the Public Broadcasting Service.

I must thank the entire staff at Palantir, the Drupal community, and, most of all, my lovely and patient wife, Amy, without whom none of this would be possible.

# Table of Contents

# Preface

This is a book about building simple web sites with Drupal—and having fun doing it. This book will enable you to build 12 exciting and simple web projects, and to create quick prototypes of commonly-used applications within hours. This book will give you a competitive edge by helping you to rapidly implement web projects for personal and business use—without having to pay a developer to do it for you. With this book, almost anyone with just a bit of Drupal knowledge can build a complex web site by mixing the individual projects together. Instant Drupal!

## What this book covers

The hands-on example projects in this book are based on fictitious web site development briefs, and they illustrate practical ways of applying Drupal. A chapter is dedicated to each example web site project. Each chapter contains a fictitious brief from which is derived the list of core and contributed modules that will be required to implement the project.

In *Chapter 1*, Isaac Meredith Smart is a professor of Sociology at Drupelburg University. His need is quite simple, and all he intends to do is to build a personal web site that will provide some shameless publicity to promote him professionally.

In *Chapter 2*, Verree High School is one of the most popular schools in Drupelburg. The school board of governors has decided to build a new web site, which will basically tell the world about the school, its facilities, and its staff.

In *Chapter 3*, The Global Hitchhikers Club is an online club for hobos and compulsive travelers. The purpose of the club web site is to enable members to keep an online blog of their travels, and provide a means for advising other club members on their own travels.

In *Chapter 4*, "Electric" Skid Jackson is a retired break-dancer and a full time choreographer and owner of the Def Freeze dance crew. Skid has an idea for a web site where all of the street dance events all over the world can be listed according to their location, so that he can be the first to know what is shaking.

In *Chapter 5*, Tony Tortilla is a student at Drupelburg University. Tony thinks that the social life could be vastly improved if the University had its own community web site where the students could get to know each other a little better.

In *Chapter 6*, The Daily Drupe is the only newspaper in Drupelburg, and it has a local circulation. The intention is to replicate the content of The Daily Drupe online, in a way that will enable the online edition to be easily updated on a real-time basis.

In *Chapter 7*, Dridgets Inc is the foremost manufacturer of bespoke widgets in Drupelburg. Their dridgets have won awards internationally and are considered to be vastly superior to other, mass-produced widgets, manufactured by so many unscrupulous garage factories. In order to consolidate their success, Dridgets have decided to set up an online e-commerce store to sell their widgets.

In *Chapter 8*, Wally Fishbourne has the idea to create an online directory where people can post details of accommodation available for rent, share, and sale all over Drupelburg. He is looking at a simple directory with listing and display features, rather in the style of Gumtree and Craigslist.

In *Chapter 9*, William and Elizabeth Bunter are organizing an online food appreciation community. They intend to enroll members from all over the world to share their food photos on a new web site, where the users will submit photos of their food for all other members to admire and rate.

In *Chapter 10*, Drupelburg Conference Venues (DCV) has been organizing conferences and events for many years. Now they think that much of their operation may be eased and much of their overheads reduced if they had a web presence. DCV is looking to create a web site where facilities can be listed and booked in real time.

In *Chapter 11*, Winston Groovy returned home to his wife Rita in Kingston Jamaica after being missing for two days, claiming to have been abducted by aliens. So Rita Groovy has decided to create a web site to aggregate occurrences of alien sightings all over the world to save other people the heartache of having their loved ones permanently lost to extra-terrestrial kidnappers.

In *Chapter 12*, bad news is always good news for the press. Vaughan Pyre has decided to take advantage of this and create a web site that will aggregate bad news and weird happenings from all over the world. The content of the site will be entirely derived from RSS feeds from several sources, with each feed being automatically retrieved and its items displayed on the web site.

In *Appendix A* you will learn to install and configure Drupal.

In *Appendix B* you will learn to optimize your Drupal site.

In *Appendix C* you will find a list of modules and themes used in this book, as well as links to their project pages.

# What you need for this book

All of the projects in this book are based on Drupal 6. A list of the contributed modules and themes employed, and links to their project pages, is provided in *Appendix C*.

# Who this book is for

This book is for anyone who wants to build a range of Drupal sites, and who wants to see how to apply the many available Drupal plugins and features in different scenarios. If you develop Drupal sites professionally, or would like to try building web sites as a freelancer, this is a great book to help you get started.

However, this book is not for absolute beginners. It is not a "dummies" book and users are advised to familiarize themselves with basic Drupal terminology and operations such as creating content, and uploading and enabling themes and modules. Some installation and configuration details are provided in the Appendix, and users are also encouraged to visit the Drupal project site (http://drupal.org) where ample help exists both in documentation and a very active users' forum.

This book will not make you an expert in developing with Drupal; it will not even bring you close. However, it should help you get your feet wet and make you unafraid to plunge deeper into the wonders of creating killer sites with a truly amazing framework.

# Conventions

In this book, you will find a number of styles of text that distinguish between different kinds of information. Here are some examples of these styles, and an explanation of their meaning.

**New terms** and **important words** are shown in bold. Words that you see on the screen, in menus or dialog boxes for example, appear in our text like this: "Click on the **edit** link in front of the vocabulary **Continent**".

[ Tips and tricks appear like this. ]

# Reader feedback

Feedback from our readers is always welcome. Let us know what you think about this book—what you liked or may have disliked. Reader feedback is important for us to develop titles that you really get the most out of.

To send us general feedback, simply send an email to feedback@packtpub.com, and mention the book title in the subject of your message.

If there is a book that you need and would like to see us publish, please send us a note in the **SUGGEST A TITLE** form on www.packtpub.com or send an email to suggest@packtpub.com.

If there is a topic that you have expertise in and you are interested in either writing or contributing to a book on, refer to author guide on www.packtpub.com/authors.

# Customer support

Now that you are the proud owner of a Packt book, we have a number of things to help you to get the most from your purchase.

# Errata

Although we have taken every care to ensure the accuracy of our contents, mistakes do happen. If you find a mistake in one of our books—maybe a mistake in text or code—we would be grateful if you would report this to us. By doing so, you can save other readers from frustration, and help us to improve subsequent versions of this book. If you find any errata, please report them by visiting http://www.packtpub.com/support, selecting your book, clicking on the **let us know** link, and entering the details of your errata. Once your errata are verified, your submission will be accepted and the errata added to any list of existing errata. Any existing errata can be viewed by selecting your title from http://www.packtpub.com/support.

# Piracy

Piracy of copyright material on the Internet is an ongoing problem across all media. At Packt, we take the protection of our copyright and licenses very seriously. If you come across any illegal copies of our works in any form on the Internet, please provide us with the location address or website name immediately so that we can pursue a remedy.

Please contact us at copyright@packtpub.com with a link to the suspected pirated material.

We appreciate your help in protecting our authors, and our ability to bring you valuable content.

# Questions

You can contact us at questions@packtpub.com if you are having a problem with any aspect of the book, and we will do our best to address it.

# 1

# I.M. Smart, Ph.D.—Building a Personal Site

Isaac Meredith Smart is a professor of Sociology at Drupelburg University.
His need is quite simple, and all he intends to do is to build a personal web site
that will provide some shameless publicity to promote him professionally. The
objective is to give his students, as well as the entire academic community, as much
information about himself as is decently permitted. Isaac wants his web site to have
the following features:

- An "About me" page—showing his personal profile and interests
- A page that will list all of his publications
- A Blog to tell the world what he is currently doing, with a list of the latest
  blog posts displayed on the front page
- A Contact form that site visitors can use to send an email to I.M. Smart

# Theme

Smart has chosen the "AD The Morning After" theme (which is a contribution to the Drupal project) because he loves the design. The front page will feature a teaser for Smart's profile at the top of the content area, and a list of his most recent blog posts in a block at the bottom of the front page. The final layout of Smart's web site can be seen in the following screenshot:

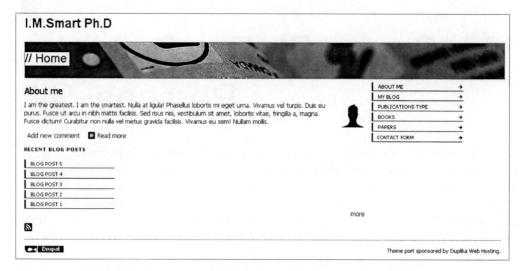

# Build I.M. Smart's site

Okay, this guy Smart doesn't appear particularly likeable does he, and isn't this quite typical of university professors? But let's put our prejudices aside for a couple of hours and get his work done for him. The major tasks in building the web site for Isaac Smart will be:

- To create a new Content type called "Publication", under which he can list all of his work
- To be able to allocate terms to describe each added work
- To be able to display a Page view of the list of publications
- To be able to create a Block view of the list of his daily blog posts
- To create a simple Contact form

# Modules

In order to create the desired web site, we will be using some essential Drupal modules.

## Optional Core modules

The following optional **Core** modules will be required:

- **Blog** — will enable him create his blog posts
- **Taxonomy** — will enable him to classify his blog posts
- **Comment** — will allow all visitors to his web site to comment on, and to discuss his blog posts and publications
- **Contact** — will allow site visitors to send him personal messages
- **Upload** — will allow the upload of files into content

## Contributed modules

The following contributed modules will also be used:

- **Taxonomy Menu** — will allow taxonomy vocabularies to be transformed into menus easily
- **IMCE** — will give the ability to upload and manage files and images
- **Image** — will allow the inclusion of images in content

# Basic content

Smart's site is quite basic. The **About Me** page can be safely created from the **Story** Content type, and that is what we are going to do. However, to add an element of danger to the project, we will be including a new Content type for his publications, and we will call it just that — "Publication".

# Create a new Content type

By navigating to the **Administer** page of the site and then to the **Content management** section, we will find the **Content types** link.

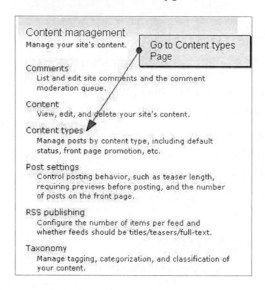

If we access this page, then we will see the various Content types listed there. Here, we need to create a new Content type for "Publication".

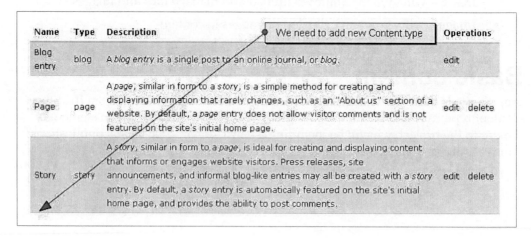

To create the "Publication" Content type:

1. Click on the **Add content type** link at the top of the page. You will then be presented with a form.

2. Add the Content type description and the general rules for the adding and display of content for this new Content type, in the places where they need to be in the form. Here are some guidelines:

   a. In the **Identification** fields, add the **Name** and the **Description** of the Content type (in this case "Publication").

   b. In the **Submission form settings**, you can choose the titles that you want to give the fields. By default, you are presented with **Title** (for the title of the submission), **Body** (for the main story), and also fields specifying the minimum length of the article before it can be accepted for submission, as well as another place where you can describe submission guidelines for this Content type. Leave this at the system default setting.

   c. In the **Workflow setting** we need to determine the default options:

      i. Do you want the article to be immediately published and available for use on the site, immediately after submission? If so, select the **Published** checkbox.

      ii. Do you want to promote the article to the front page? If so, select the **Promoted to front page** checkbox.

      iii. Do you want the article to remain at the top of the list of contents on the site? If so, select the **Sticky at top of list** checkbox.

   d. In the **Comments settings** panel, indicate whether you want to allow comments to be made on articles of this Content type or not, and if you do, how these comments will be handled. As previously mentioned, Smart wants to allow comments to be added to his publications by site visitors.

# Categorize content

We first need to establish how the content is going to be organized for use on the site. This is quite easy because we have created only one new Content type, named **Publication**, that will have taxonomy terms—**Books** and **Papers**—attached to it. By doing this, we will have set the ground rules for how content will be created and displayed on the site.

Categories or terms may be used to further classify items that, even though they fall under the same Content type, need to be grouped with others with which they bear a close similarity. In this case, Smart's Publication list includes **Books** and **Papers**, which, even though they are both publications, would do well if grouped separately. So we must now create the new categories and establish relationships between these new categories and the new Content type.

Go to the **Taxonomy** link under the **Content management** section on the **Administer** page, and click on it to get to the Taxonomy page. If you have started a new site, then at the foot of this page, you will see a notice that there is no vocabulary available for your new categories. The **vocabulary** is a term by which a collection of categories (or terms) can be collectively described. In this case, let us create a vocabulary that we will call **Publications Type**. We will do this by clicking on the **Add vocabulary** link at the top of the page. This is what we will be entering into the form for this new vocabulary:

1. In the **Identification** panel, let us enter the **Vocabulary name**, and a **Description**, as well as any **Help text** that will guide Smart when he comes across this vocabulary. For **Publication**, we have used **Publications Type** as the **Vocabulary name**. For the **Description**, we have entered **The type of publication. Is it book or paper?** For the **Help text**, we will be instructing Smart to **Select appropriate publication**.

2. We need to associate this vocabulary with a **Content type**. We have created it specifically for **Publication**, so we will naturally select the **Publication** checkbox.

3. For the **Settings**, we declare that the selection of a term from this vocabulary is **Required**, and that Smart must choose a term from the supplied list. Moreover, because a Publication can be either a Book or a Paper but never both, a posted content may not have more than one term associated with it. Therefore, leave all of the other checkboxes with the system default settings.

The completed vocabulary page is shown in the following screenshot:

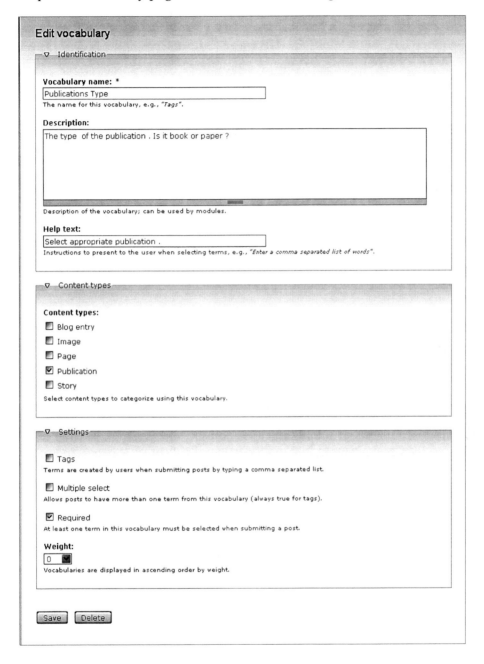

On returning to the **Taxonomy** page, we can see the new vocabulary that we have just created is listed. Now we need to add the terms for the vocabulary. We do this by clicking on the **add terms** link and completing the form that we will be presented with. At this stage, forget about the **Advanced Options** link at the bottom, because we only have a single level of terms.

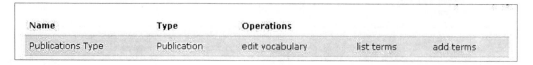

| Name | Type | Operations | | |
|------|------|-----------|---|---|
| Publications Type | Publication | edit vocabulary | list terms | add terms |

If you click on the **list terms** link on the vocabulary, then you will be presented with a list of the terms that you have created, in the order that these terms will be presented to Smart. If you don't like this order, then just drag the ones you want to change to the location that you want.

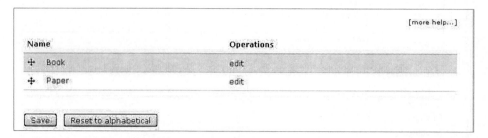

[more help...]

| Name | Operations |
|------|-----------|
| ✛ Book | edit |
| ✛ Paper | edit |

[ Save ]  [ Reset to alphabetical ]

# Test the submission form

Now, let us test our content submission form and see how it works. In order to do this, you click on the **Create content** link (on the lefthand side of your page), and select **Publication**. You will then get a form, as shown in the following screenshot:

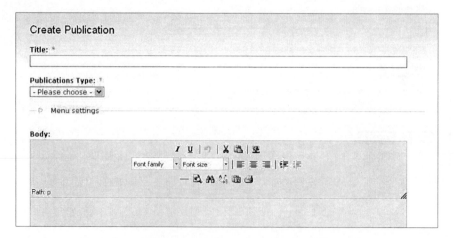

Using this form, Smart will be able to post the details of his many publications to his web site. However, he doesn't know a thing about HTML (which proves that he isn't so great after all) and will definitely have problems while uploading images into his posts. So, we will give him an easy way to do this.

# Images

Download the **IMCE** and **Image** modules. Install and enable them. It is also essential that you have the **Upload** module enabled. The **TinyMCE** editor (even though it is not essential) will permit Smart to edit his pages without knowing any HTML. Download the editor, if this feature is required.

Having done this, return to **Administer | Content management | Content types**, and select the **Publication** Content type. At the bottom of the page, you will see a new panel for **Image Attach settings**. Enable **Attach images**, and now the **Publication** Content type will be ready to incorporate images. To confirm this, go to the **Create content** link for the Content type. Near the bottom of the page you will find the **Attached images** panel, as shown in the following screenshot, where you can upload images for your content. Do the same for the **Blog entry**, **Story**, and **Page** Content types.

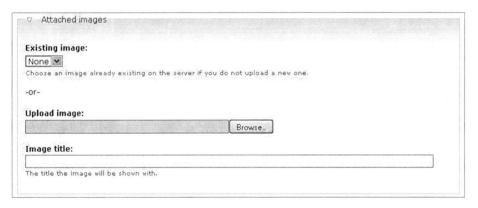

If you have configured your **TinyMCE** editor correctly, then you can similarly post images into the **Body** of your article by using the image upload function in TinyMCE.

We will also ensure that the **Attach images** functionality has been enabled in all of the other Content types. Then, in the **Workflow settings** for each Content type, deselect the **Promoted to front page** checkbox, or else you will end up with a very unruly front page display.

# Create the About Me page

The **About Me** page, as we have decided, should really be quite straightforward and will be created from the **Story** Content type, which is recommended for content that is static.

1. From the **admin** menu, click on the **Create content** link, and then select **Story**. This will give you a form, which is similar to the following screenshot:

2. The handy **WYSIWYG (What You See Is What You Get)** editor, which is an emulation of desktop software like MS Word or Open Doc (with which most people will probably be accustomed), will make it easy for Smart to create his personal information page, and format it to his satisfaction.

**Tips and traps**

We have used this approach because Smart is the only person having a personal profile on this web site. Otherwise, it will not be adequate, and we may have to call up some other modules, especially the CCK module, which will enable us to create new form fields to make submissions more intuitive (for example, to present defined fields for name, education, interests, and so on).

3. Because Smart wants this to feature on the front page, we will just promote the **About Me** page to the front page before saving it. The **Menu settings** field is optional, and it is only used if you want to add the item to the menu system. We will add the **About Me** page to the **<Primary links>**.

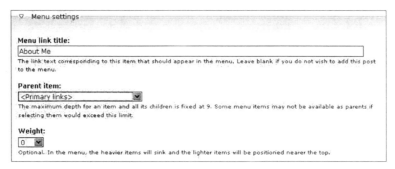

# Create Blog posts

Blog posts will be created in the same way as the other Content types.

Click on the **Create content** link on the **admin** menu and select **Blog entry**. This will give you a form similar to the one that we have used to create the **About Me** page. Smart will be able to type in his blog posts and save them. This is so very easy!

# Create a Publication

Publications will also be created from the **Publication** Content type.

1.  Click on the **Create content** link in the **admin** menu, and select **Publication**. This will give you a form similar to the following screenshot:

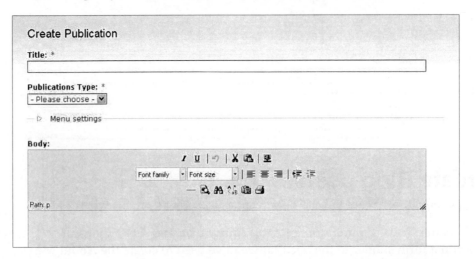

2.  Select the type of publication that you are creating from the **Publications Type** drop–down list. Again, with the handy WYSIWYG editor, adding content is very easy.

# Create a Contact form

Having enabled the **Contact** module, we will now configure this to send messages to Smart at his email address `iamsmart@drupelburg.edu`.

1.  Go to the **Administer** page and select the **Contact form** link.
2.  In the **Contact form** page, add a new category to the form and name it **Website Feedback** (or whatever you want). Also, enter Smart's email as the recipient.

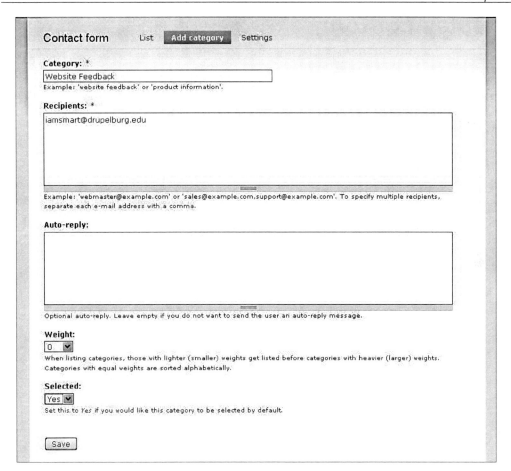

3. The URL for the **Contact form** will be `http://www.sitename.com/?q=contact`. We will be adding this link to the menu later.

# Display content

Now comes the fun part of nicely displaying the content for viewing.

# Create quick menus with the Taxonomy Menu module

Now that we have learned much of what is required to post content into Smart's web site, let's take a look at how we may view the content that we have put in. Again, there are several ways to do this. My favorite "quick and easy way" is to use a module known as the **Taxonomy Menu**. What this essentially does is permits you to view the content on your site just by clicking on a menu link that corresponds to the title of a vocabulary term. Select the vocabularies that you want to include in your menu, and save the configuration. You will now see the links to items related to each vocabulary under the Navigation menu in the sidebar.

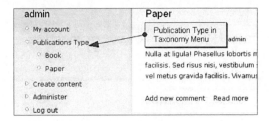

# Menus

We now have all of our pages as Smart would want them, but the navigation could still be improved. What we are going to do next is to arrange all of the menu items so that they are easily accessible. To do this, we will have to visit the **Menus** link on the **Administer** page, which will bring us to the page shown in the following screenshot:

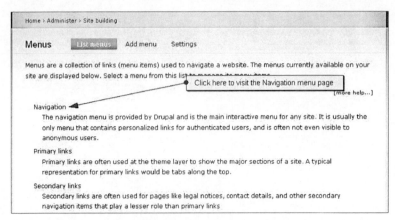

What we intend to do is to move all of the menu links of the site content pages, as well as the **Contact form** page under the **Primary links** menu. At the moment, most of them are still under **Navigation**. So let us visit the **Navigation** menu page.

1. Click on the **edit** operation in front of **Publications Type**, and when you get to the edit page, change the **Parent item** to **<Primary links>**.

2. Do the same for **My blog**. We will end up with a view of the page, as shown in the following screenshot:

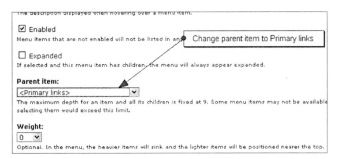

3. There is one last item that we need to add, and that is the **Contact form**. Click on the **Add item** tab at the top of the **Primary links** page. You will be asked to define the **Path**, **Menu link title**, and **Parent item** of the **Contact form**. Set these as **contact** (as indicated while creating the contact form), **Contact form**, and select **<Primary links>** respectively. The completed form is shown in the following screenshot:

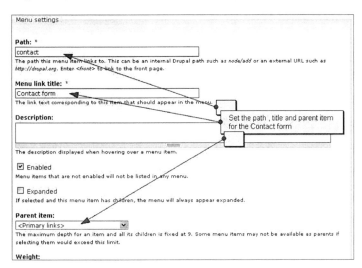

When you are finally returned to the **Primary links** page, you have the opportunity to rearrange all of the menu items as you wish by dragging them to the desired positions.

# Latest blog posts

Smart wants a list of his latest blog posts to be shown on the front page. Doing this is a lot easier than you might think. Let's visit the **Blocks** page, by going to the **Blocks** link on the **Administer** page. We will see that a block already exists for **Recent blog posts**. Drag it to a position under **Content**. However, this will make the latest blog posts to show on all of the pages, despite the fact that Smart only wants them on the front page. So we will need to configure this block to show only on the first page. Click on the **configure** operation in front of the block, and for the **Page specific visibility settings**, enter **node**.

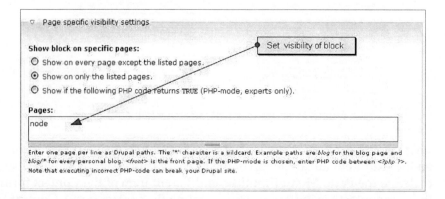

While we are on the Blocks page, let's also drag the **Primary links** block to the **Left sidebar** (where we want it in our theme). The **Block title** of the block can be set to **<none>** to remove the default **Primary links** title.

As IM Smart wouldn't allow anyone else to log in to his web site we could also disable the login form, by removing by setting the **Region** of the **User login** block to **<none>**, and then click on the **Save** button, at the bottom of the page, to finish.

# Permissions

A couple of details still need to be sorted out. We have created the content, but as it presently is, not the entire site is visible to everyone, especially the **Contact form**. We must set these permissions via the **Permissions** link on the **Administer** page. Make the **access site-wide contact form** permission accessible to all roles. Now, let us visit the front page to see what we have so far.

# Finishing up

Smart has chosen the **AD The Morning After** theme to make his site more interesting. So we will now upload the theme and enable it.

The theme, once applied, confirms that all of the work required for I. M. Smart's site is finally done.

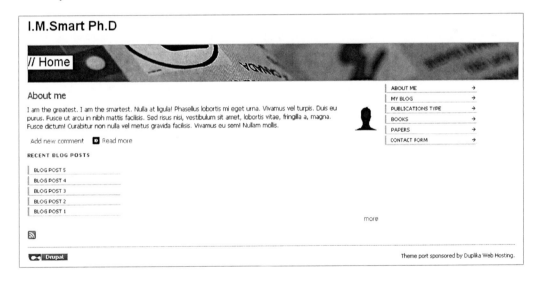

# Summary

In this chapter, you have learned how to:

- Build a basic site for any purpose
- Create new Content types and vocabularies
- Organize your content for display, using the Core **Menu** module and also the **Taxonomy** module

In real life, you may have more Content types and more content pages that are linked to the menu, such as the "About Me" page and a larger number of content categories, but the procedure basically remains the same.

# 2

# Verree High School—Building a School Site

Verree High School is one of the most popular schools in Drupelburg. The school Board of Governors has decided to build a new web site that will basically tell the world about the school, its facilities, and its staff. The web site should be able to keep the world informed about the school's many activities, and it should also include a simple application form, through which detailed admission enquiries can be made. A page should also be included from which documents such as syllabuses and brochures can be downloaded.

Verree High School needs to incorporate the following features into their new web site:

- Content pages with the following descriptions:
    ○ Front page (About our School)
    ○ Our facilities
    ○ Our vision and mission
- A web-enabled application form for prospective students to make specific inquiries
- A page to list all of the downloadable items (brochures, catalogs, and so on)

# Theme

The theme chosen for this project (for no particular reason) is "Beginning", which is a Drupal community contribution. The front page will feature a three-column theme.

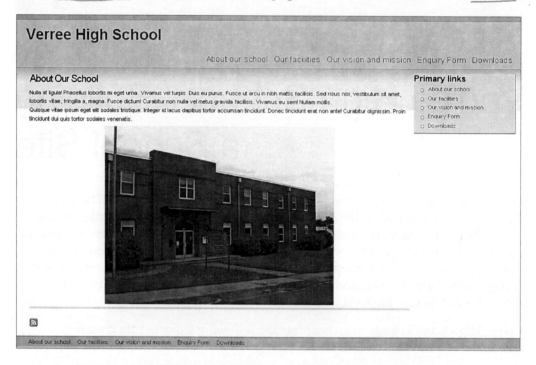

# Build the Verree High School site

The Verree High School web site is actually a simple site mostly made up of static pages such as **About our School**, **Our facilities**, and **Our vision and mission**. The complications that have been introduced into what otherwise would have been a straightforward site, which could have been completed within a couple of hours, are:

- A web-enabled form for detailed enquiries from the site users
- A download summary page where brochures and other files available to users may easily be accessed

# Modules

From the tasks that are presented by this project, we are able to compile a list of contributed modules that will be used. So, for the purpose of this example, we shall be using the following modules:

## Optional Core modules

The following modules are part of the Drupal Core and are not enabled by default. However, we need to use them:

- **Taxonomy**—enables us to classify our content
- **Upload**—allows the upload of files and images into content

## Contributed modules

The following modules are not a part of the Drupal Core. We will have to obtain and upload them for use in this project.

- **Webform**—allows the creation of web-enabled forms for use on this project.
- **Views**—allows you to create customized lists and queries from your database.
- **Simpleviews**—an easy-to-use tool for building content listing pages.
- **Image**—allows users with the correct permissions to upload images. Thumbnails and additional sized images are created automatically.
- **IMCE**—gives the client the ability to upload and manage some files through the Admin interface.
- **Taxonomy Menu**—easily transforms taxonomy vocabularies into menus.
- **TinyMCE**—makes the formatting of all articles easier.

## Enable modules

First, visit the **Modules** page and enable all of the modules that we need. For simplicity, just select all of the checkboxes related to the modules listed above. It is especially important to enable the **Upload** and **Webform** modules.

# Configure the Webform module

We must configure the **Webform** module exactly as we want it to work. For this, visit the link or the page for the **Webform** module on the **Administer** page, and you will be shown the following page.

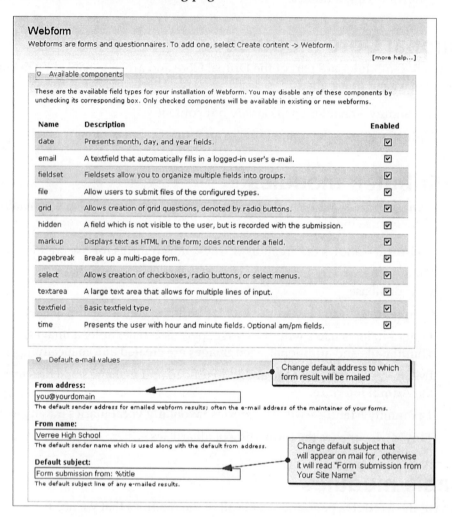

All that is actually necessary to do is to change the default email to the one via which you will want submitted forms to be sent, and specify the default title of the form by which submissions are sent. Having done this, the **Webform** module will now be configured for use.

# Configure the File uploads module

The **Upload** module should also be configured if you are intending to upload a file of an unusual format. Go to the **File uploads** link on the **Administer** page, and you will be presented with the page shown in the following screenshot:

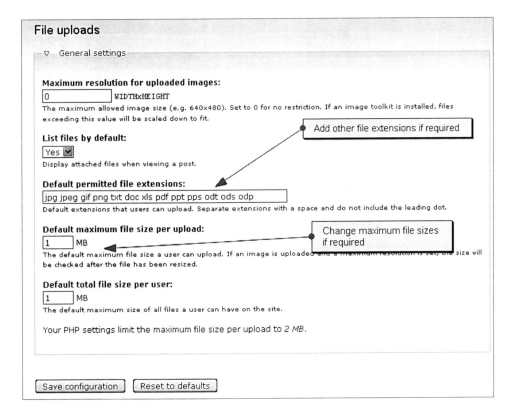

Make the relevant changes according to your liking, especially if you need to add more file extension types to the default permitted file extensions, or if you need to change the maximum file size that is permitted. Otherwise, leave the default settings intact, and save the page. However, be conscious of the security issues of permitting executable files to be uploaded.

# Create the Downloads Content type

By browsing to the **Administer** page of the site and then into the **Content management** section (shown in the following screenshot), we will find the **Content types** link. If we access this page, then we will see the various **Content types** listed there.

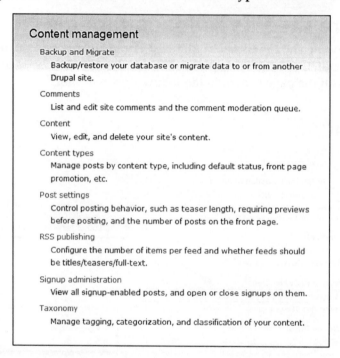

Here, we need to create a new Content type for "Downloads", as this will make it easier for the site administrator to post files for downloading.

| Name | Type | Description | Operations |
|------|------|-------------|------------|
| Image | image | An image (with thumbnail). This is ideal for publishing photographs or screenshots. | edit |
| Page | page | A *page*, similar in form to a *story*, is a simple method for creating and displaying information that rarely changes, such as of a website. By default, a *page* entry does not allow and is not featured on the site's initial home page. | edit |
| Story | story | A *story*, similar in form to a *page*, is ideal for creating and displaying content that informs or engages website visitors. Press releases, site announcements, and informal blog-like entries may all be created with a *story* entry. By default, a *story* entry is automatically featured on the site's initial home page, and provides the ability to post comments. | edit  delete |
| Webform | webform | Create a new form or questionnaire accessible to users. Submission results and statistics are recorded and accessible to privileged users. | edit |

We need to add another content type "Downloads"

To create the "Downloads" Content type:

1. Click on the **Add content type** link at the top of the page. You will then be presented with a form.

2. Add the Content type descriptions, the general rules for the adding of content, and the display of content for this new Content type, in the places where they need to be in the form. Here are some guidelines:

   a. In the **Identification** fields, enter the **Name** and **Description** of the content type—**Downloads**.

   b. In the **Submission form settings**, choose the title that you want to give the fields. By default, you are presented with **Title** (for the title of the submission), **Body** (for the main story), and also the fields demanding the minimum length of an article before it can be accepted for submission. A field where you can describe submission guidelines for this Content type can also be found here (leave this at the system default setting).

   c. In the **Workflow setting**, we need to determine the default options:

      ◦ Do you want the article to be published and made available for use on the site immediately after submission? If so, select the **Published** checkbox.

      ◦ Do you want to promote the article to the front page? If so, select the **Promoted to front page** checkbox.

      ◦ Do you want the article to remain at the top of the list of contents on the site? If so, select the **Sticky at top of list** checkbox.

      ◦ In the **Attachments** option, select **Enabled**, in order to permit downloadable files to be attached to the content.

   d. In the **Comment Settings**, you can indicate whether you want to allow comments to be made on articles from this Content type or not, and if you do, then how these comments will be handled.

   e. In the **Image Attach settings**, enable **Attach Images**, so that images can also be added to the text.

Perform the steps c to e for each of the other Content types.

# Handle attachments and images

Go to the **Create content** link for **Downloads** or any of the other Content types. Near the bottom end of the page, you will find the **Attached Image** panel (where you can upload images to go with your text) and the **File attachments** panel.

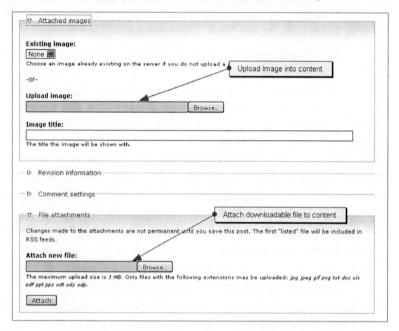

If you have also configured your TinyMCE editor correctly, then you should have an editor bar, similar to the one shown in the following screenshot, in the **Body** field. You can similarly post images into the body of your text content by using the image upload function in the TinyMCE editor. You may, however, use any other text editor of your choice (for example, FCKeditor), which will of course result in a different but functionally-similar editor bar.

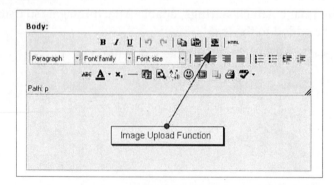

# Test the Downloads submission form

Now let us test our **Downloads** submission form and see how it works. To do this, click on the **Create content** link on the lefthand side of the page, and select **Downloads**. You will then get a form similar to the following screenshot:

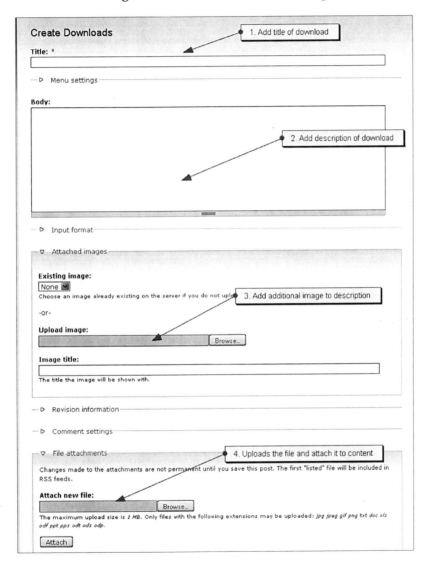

Add one or two pages, and post some files to make sure that your file upload function has been set up properly. You should end up with a typical downloadable file content page as shown in the following screenshot:

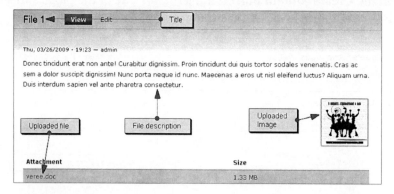

# Create a Webform

Every form that is created by using this module is actually a new Drupal node. The first form that we will be presented with, when creating a Webform, is the **Site configuration** (settings) page that will tell Drupal how to handle your completed form.

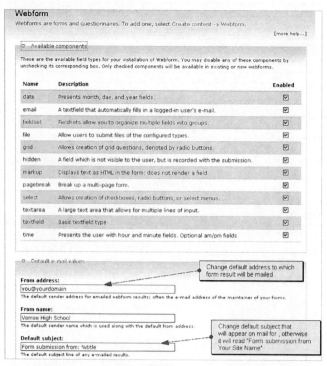

For the purpose of this web site, we are required to create a simple **Enquiry Form**, which will capture the following information from the visitor:

- Name
- Email
- Telephone
- Gender
- Date of Birth
- Interests

Webform is a very powerful module that can be configured to do amazing things, depending on the components of the module that are used when creating the form. The example that we are attempting to perform, barely scratches the surface of the abilities of this module. Therefore, we will actually be performing very minor configurations.

As usual, we are able to create a Webform by visiting the **Create content** link and selecting **Webform**. There are some parameters that need to be defined, such as:

- The title of the form and a description, if available
- Whether the form will give a confirmatory message on submission, or direct the submitter to a URL that you have provided
- Whether the form will be emailed to an address that you have supplied, or the result will be accessed online by permitted users

For our form, we have used the following parameters:

- **Title: Enquiry Form**
- **Description: To make enquiries from Verree High School**
- **Confirmation Message: Thank you for your message**
- **Email to Address: enquiry@verreehigh.com**

The Webform with all the parameters filled in is shown in the following screenshot:

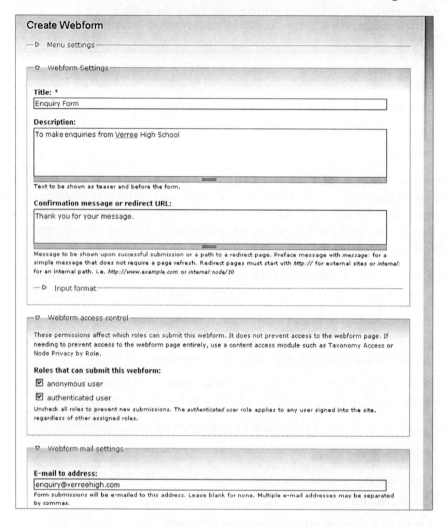

The other settings can be left with their default values. Now we can click on the **Save** button. Upon saving the Webform, we are taken to another page, from which we actually begin to build our form.

All of the information field that we require from the form user will be created from a component that relates to the type of data required. Specifically:

- **Name** – requires a **textfield** type component.
- **Email** – requires an **email** type component.
- **Telephone** – requires a **textfield** type component.

- **Gender** — requires a **select** type component
- **Date of Birth** — requires a **date** type component
- **Interest** — requires a **textarea** type component

These are the only components that we will use to build our **Enquiry Form**.

**Tips and traps**

When creating the **Enquiry Form**, make sure that the TinyMCE editor has been disabled on the page. Failing to do so may result in unnecessary HTML tags being applied to the text appearing in the text fields.

# Create Name field

To create the **Name** field, we enter **Name** as the field **Name**, select **textfield** as the **Type**, and then click on the **Add** button.

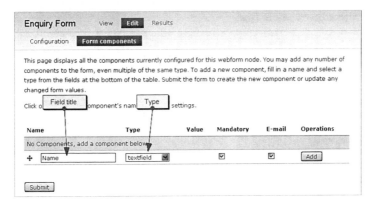

This takes us to another form, which will permit us to add more information about this field, as shown in the following screenshot:

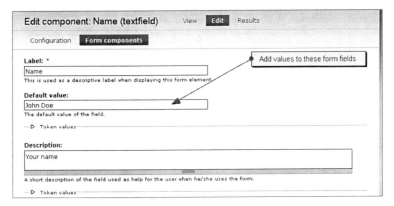

Here we have added:

1. **Label** — the label of the field, which will be **Name,** as shown in the previous screenshot.
2. **Default value** — some dummy data that will make the addition of a value to this field by the user a more intuitive process. In our case, we have entered **John Doe**.

Leave all of the other settings with their default values, and then click on the **Submit** button.

The **Telephone** field is created using a similar procedure.

# Create an Email field

The **Email** field is built in a similar way to the **Name** field that we have just created, but with a different Webform component. The **Email** field can be configured as shown in the following screenshot:

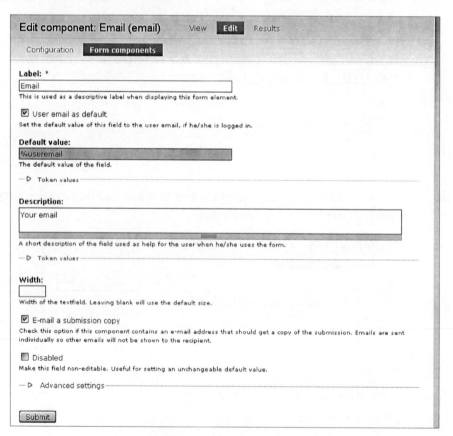

In the configuration form that we have seen, a couple of new parameters will have to be defined. These parameters are:

- Whether the user's email will be the default email to be used in this field
- Whether a copy of the submitted form should be emailed to this user

# Create a Gender field

The **Gender** field is also built in a similar way to the other two fields, but with a different component. For this field, we will be using the **Select** component. Therefore, we will need to present options to the user to select from. The values to be entered for this field are shown in the following screenshot:

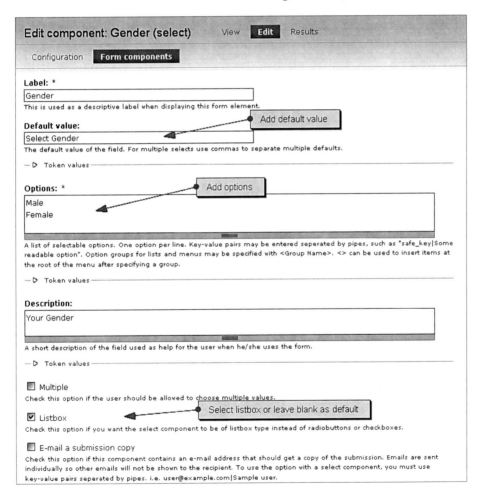

Additionally, we need to determine how this field will be presented to the user — as a listbox or as a checkbox. We will also determine whether multiple values are permitted. Thankfully, in this case, our user will be (hopefully) either male or female.

# Create the Date of Birth field

The **Date of Birth** field is created using the **date** component. The following screenshot shows the values to be entered:

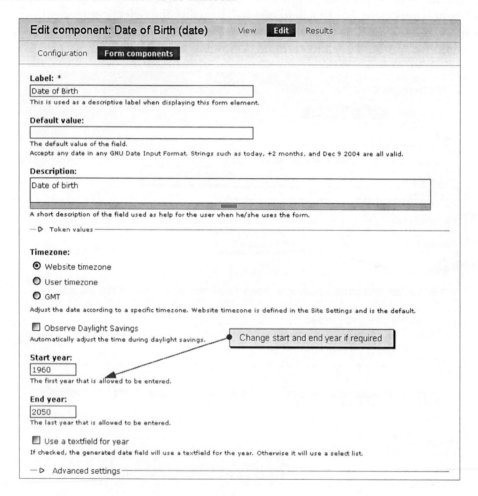

The main settings in this form are the **Timezone**, the **Start year**, and the **End year** for the field. Most of these do not really affect the result of the form.

# Create the Interest field

The **Interest** field uses the **textarea** component, because this component can better handle content of undetermined length. The completed **Interest** field is shown in the following screenshot:

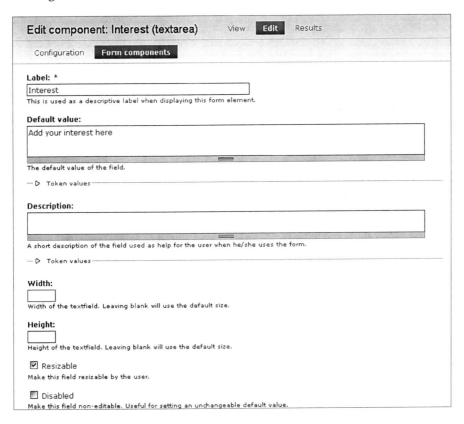

Most of the settings here can be kept safely with their default values.

# View the Form

Now, in order to see what our completed form looks like, click on the **View** tab at the top of the page to which we are adding the components. The result can be seen in the following screenshot:

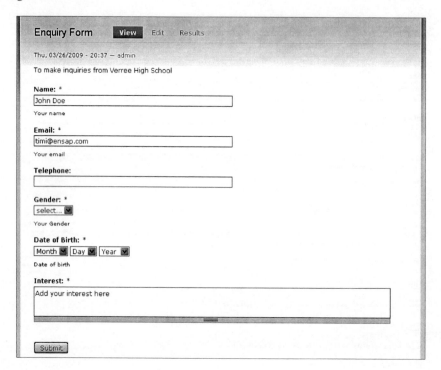

Looks nice doesn't it?

**Tips and traps**

Remember to change the permissions for the users (to create or view file uploads, create or view images, and view the Webform) in the **Permissions** link on the **Administer** page.

# Display content

The Downloads summary page lists all of the content submitted under the **Downloads** Content type. This page will make it easy for users to quickly locate items that are available for download.

## Downloads summary Page

In order to create this page, enable the **SimpleViews** and **View** modules. Visit the configuration page for the **SimpleViews** module at **Administer | Site building | Simple views**. Click on the **Add view** tab, and create a view for the **Download list** page by entering the configurations shown in the following screenshot:

This will create a page view and a block for the items that have been posted under the **Downloads** Content type.

## Create Menus

Now let's tidy up our site by creating a menu system that is more intuitive. We want to have the ability to access all of our content pages from under the **Primary links** menu. In order to do this, go to the individual content pages that you have created (**About our school**, **Our facilities**, **Our vision and mission**, **Enquiry Form**), and click on the **Edit** tab.

In the menu setting for each content page, add a menu title and set the **Parent item** as **<Primary links>**.

 **Tips and traps**

You could have also done this at the time of creating your content.

Now go to **Menus** link on the **Administer** page. Select the **Add item** tab in the **Primary links** menu page, and add the page URL for the **Downloads** page to the **<Primary links>** as shown in the following screenshot:

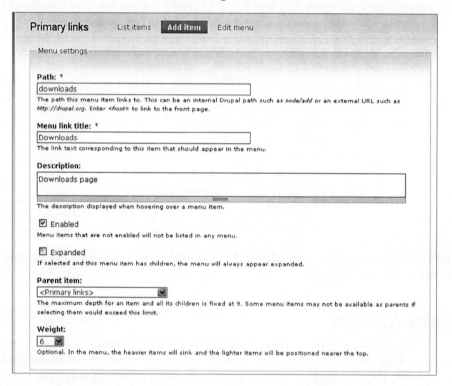

When we have completed this, let us visit the **Blocks** link on the **Administer** page, and move the **Primary links** block to the **Right sidebar** — where we want it.

On this page, you may also opt to remove the **User login** and the **Navigation** blocks from the sidebar.

# Finishing up

We may now enable our new theme, **Beginning**, on the **Themes** page, and configure it to our preferences. Verree High School now has a website that satisfies the needs of the Board of Governors.

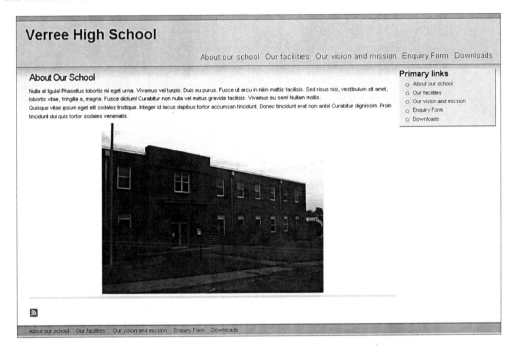

# Summary

In this chapter, you have learned how to:

- Build a basic site for a small educational, research, or non-profit organization
- Use the **Webform** module to create dynamic forms and questionnaires
- Use the **SimpleViews** and **Views** modules to generate quick page and block views of content by Content type

# 3

# Global Hitchhikers Club— Building an Aficionado's Site

The Global Hitchhikers Club is an online club for hobos and compulsive travelers. The purpose of the club web site is to enable members to keep an online blog of their travels, and to provide a means for advising other club members on their own travels. In their blog, club members will describe the places where they've been, including the sleeping and eating facilities, as well as the disposition of the natives. Users can also upload photos.

The Global Hitchhikers Club web site will have the following distinguishing features:

- Members will be able to create their own profile page, which will be visible to other members
- Members will be able to create blog entries, categorized by the continent location, and be able to upload photos into these entries
- The latest blog entries will automatically be promoted to the front page
- Site users will be able to comment on these blog entries

Links will be provided to show page views of blog entries categorized by continent.

# Theme

The theme chosen for the Global Hitchhikers Club web site is "Pushbutton", which is a Drupal core theme. The front page will feature a two-column layout.

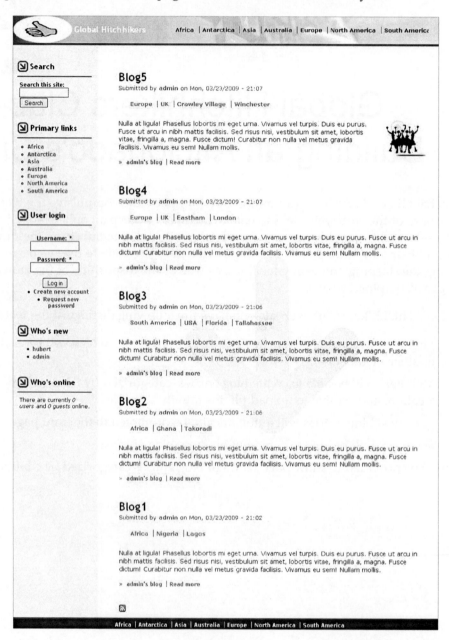

# Build the Global Hitchhikers Club site

Picture Hubert the hobo, sitting on a park bench in central Timbuktu, with his trusty laptop beside him. After locating a free Wi-Fi hotspot, he proceeds to report back to the rest of the club via the web site about his journey so far, his present location, how he successfully completed his travel, and the best way to get free amenities such as free meals and liquor at his destination.

In order to enable this web site to function successfully, we need to do the following:

- Select the modules necessary to implement the required functionalities and configure them

- Establish profile pages where members may fully describe themselves and where other members can track their travels (profile pages will contain name, email, mobile phone number, age, gender, and nationality)

- Create selectable terms for Hubert to describe the continent where he has found himself

- Create form fields for him to tag his specific location — country and locality

- Categorize and organize all of the content in a logical way, to enable it to be easily accessed and read

# Modules

From the tasks that are presented by this project, we are able to build a list of contributed modules that will be used.

## Optional Core modules

Now, there are often several ways of getting the same result. Each method undoubtedly requires different combinations of contributed and Core modules. However, for the purpose of this example, we shall be using the following **Core** modules:

- **Taxonomy** — enables us to classify our content
- **Comment** — permits users to comment on stories
- **Upload** — allows the upload of files and images into content
- **Profile** — allows the configuration of user profiles
- **Blog** — enables the easy and regular update of web pages and blog posts
- **Search** — enables site-wide searches by keyword

## Contributed modules

The following modules will have to be obtained and uploaded for use in this project:

- **Image** — allows users with the correct permissions to upload images. Thumbnails and additional sizes of images are created automatically.
- **IMCE** — gives the client the ability to upload and manage some files through the Admin interface.
- **Taxonomy Menu** — easily transforms taxonomy vocabularies into menus.
- **TinyMCE** — makes adding page breaks and setting a drop cap in the articles a bit easier. We have most of the buttons disabled.

## Basic content

As the site is built around the **Blog** module, no other Content type will need to be created. However, the main challenge that will still present itself is how to categorize the content in a way that will make it useable. But before we do this, let us first define the users and how they will be registered and visible to others.

# User settings

The basic user settings may be found as a link on the **Administer** page, and the page to which it opens to is called **User settings** (surprise). Let us enable **Signatures** at the bottom of this page (so that members can add cool sign-offs at the end of their blogs, like Namaste, Adios amigos, Peace brothers, Ketchya, Yours Truly, Sayonara, Wha' Gwan, and so on). Let us also enable picture support (so that members can have their pictures displayed in their profiles).

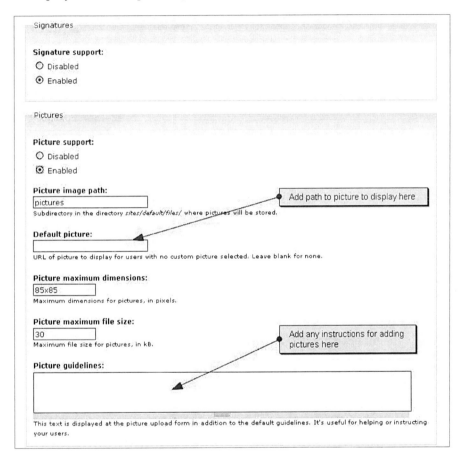

# User profile

However, what we have done so far will not give us a user profile page that is comprehensive enough. To get what we want, we need to enable the **Profile** module on the modules page. On visiting the **Profiles** link in the **admin** menu, we will be presented with a page like the following:

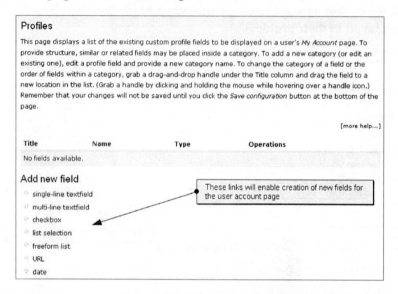

This page presents us with seven possibilities for creating new fields on the **User account** page. Now let us add form fields for the following information:

- Username
- Alternate email address
- Mobile phone
- Date of birth
- Gender

# Name

The **Name** field is a **single-line textfield**. This is the link on the **Profiles** page that we will click on to create this field. This gives us a page where we will fill in the following details:

- In the **Category** field, let us enter **Personal information**, because that is exactly what this is all about.
- For the **Title**, enter **Name**.

- For the **Form name**, enter **profile_name**.
- For **Visibility**, select **Public field, content shown on profile page but not used on member list pages**.
- For the **Page title**, enter **People whose name is %value**. This will enable site users to find people whose name contains a certain string defined by the user (for example, Tom, Tomas).
- Select the last three checkboxes to make this field compulsory, auto-completed, and visible when users are newly registering.

The completed page is shown in the following screenshot:

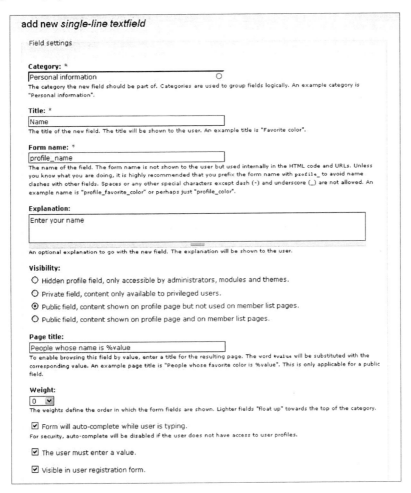

The **Alternate email address** and **Mobile Phone** fields are created by using a similar method.

# Date of Birth

The **Date of Birth** field is a **date** field, so that is the link that we will click on to create this field.

- In the **Category** field, let us enter **Personal information** because that is exactly what this is all about
- For the **Title,** enter **Date of Birth**
- For the **Form** name, enter **profile_dob**
- For **Visibility,**select **Public field, content shown on profile page but not used on member list pages**
- For the **Page title,** enter **People whose birthday is %value**
- Select the last three checkboxes to make this field compulsory, auto-completed, and visible when users are newly registering

# Gender

The **Gender** field is a **list selection,** because each blogger is either male, or female. Okay, we'll add the **I don't know** category for political correctness.

- In the **Category** field, let us enter **Personal information** because that is exactly what this is all about
- For the **Title**, enter **Gender**
- For the **Form name**, enter **profile_gender**
- For **Selection options**, enter **Male, Female,** and **I don't know,** on separate lines
- For **Visibility**, select **Public field, content shown on profile page but not used on member list page**
- For the **Page title**, enter **People whose gender is %value**
- Select all of the last three checkboxes to make this field compulsory, auto-completed and visible when users are newly registering

The following screenshot shows how our new profile creation page looks:

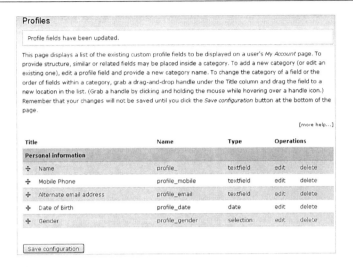

Save the configuration. Note that we have chosen to have all of these fields show on the user registration page. In order to make sure that it works the way we planned, let's log out from our **admin** account for a minute and attempt to register as a new user, by clicking on the **Create new account** link. The form that will be presented to us will be similar to the one shown in following screenshot:

So our profile page has been properly configured (the way we want it), and you can finally see what happens when Hubert completes his profile.

# Configure the Blog entry Content type

The **Blog entry** Content type is automatically created when the core **Blog** module is enabled. This Content type will permit users to post blog posts that are simply user journals.

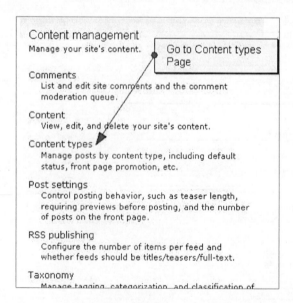

Ensure that you have enabled the **Blog** module. When we go onto the **Administer** page of the site, and then onto the **Content management** section, we will find the **Content types** link. If we access this page, then we will see the various Content types listed there.

Content types    **List**    Add content type

Below is a list of all the content types on your site. All posts that exist on your site are instances of one of these content types.

| Name | Type | Description | Operations |
|------|------|-------------|------------|
| Blog entry | blog | A *blog entry* is a single post to an online journal, or *blog*. | edit |
| Page | page | A *page*, similar in form to a *story*, is a simple method for creating and displaying information that rarely changes, such as an "About us" section of a website. By default, a *page* entry does not allow visitor comments and is not featured on the site's initial home page. | edit  delete |
| Story | story | A *story*, similar in form to a *page*, is ideal for creating and displaying content that informs or engages website visitors. Press releases, site announcements, and informal blog-like entries may all be created with a *story* entry. By default, a *story* entry is automatically featured on the site's initial home page, and provides the ability to post comments. | edit  delete |

We will not be creating a new Content type, as the **Blog entry** Content type is already present.

1. Click on the **edit** link for the **Blog entry** Content type. You will then be presented with a form.

2. In the **Workflow setting** panel, we need to determine the default options:

   ° Do you want the blog entry published and available for use on the site immediately after submission? If so, select the **Published** checkbox.

   ° Do you want the blog entry to be promoted to the front page? If so, select the **Promoted to front page** checkbox.

   ° Do you want the blog entry to remain at the top of the list of contents on the site? If so, select the **Sticky at top of list** checkbox. For this project, we should probably ignore this option.

3. In the **Comments settings** panel, you can indicate whether you want to allow comments to be posted for blog entries or not, and if you do, how these comments will be handled. For our example, we will allow comments to be made on blog entries.

# Images

You may have seen that the form has no place to enable us to add images. Therefore, Hubert the hobo cannot post images into his blog entries, as he does not know how to code HTML.

Download the **IMCE** and **Image** modules, and install and enable them. While at it, also download the TinyMCE editor, enable it, and configure it. The TinyMCE editor is not essential, though. If it is not included, then Hubert might need to learn how to code after all, in order to be able to insert pictures, tables, and formatted text inline in his blog entries. Finally, you must also enable the **Upload** module, or else no user will be able to attach images or other files to their blog entries.

Having done this, return to **Administer | Content management | Content types**, and display the **Blog entry** Content type page again. At the bottom of the page, you will see a new panel for **Image Attach settings**. Enable **Attach images**, and now your blog entries will be ready to incorporate images. In order to confirm this, go to the **Create content** link for the **Blog entry** Content type again. Near the bottom, you will find the **Attached images** panel, where you can upload images to your blog entries.

For these to work though, you need to set the user permissions to enable your registered users to use the functionalities mentioned above.

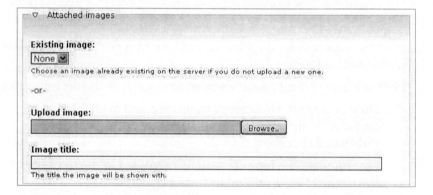

You may find that the **TinyMCE WYSIWYG editor** module may be quite difficult to configure all by itself. For this, there is also an **autoconf** module that does much of the hard work for you, automatically.

If you have configured your TinyMCE editor correctly, then you should have an editor toolbar, similar to the one shown in the following screenshot, in the **Body** text area. You can similarly post images onto the body of your blogs by using the image upload function in your TinyMCE editor, as well as add formatting to the **Body** text, by using the text formatting function.

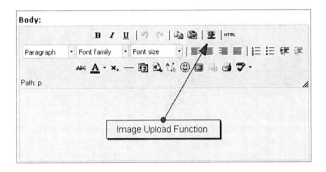

# Create new categories

Our blog entries will need to be organized into categories in order to group them together with other blog entries, according to geographical location.

Go to the **Taxonomy** link under **Content management** section in the **Administer** page, and navigate to the Taxonomy page. If you have started a new site, then you will see at the foot of this page a notice that there is no vocabulary available for your new categories. The **vocabulary** is a term by which a collection of categories (or terms) can be collectively described. In this case, let us create three vocabularies—Continent, Country, and Location. We will do this by clicking on the **Add Vocabulary** link at the top of the page. The form for this new vocabulary will then be filled with the following values:

1.  In the **Identification** panel, let us enter the name of the vocabulary, a **Description**, and also any **Help text** that comes to mind to guide the users when they come across this vocabulary. For Continent, we have used **Continent** as the **Vocabulary name**. For the **Description,** we have entered **The continent that you are posting from**, and for the **Help text,** we will be instructing the user to **Enter the continent which you are posting from**.

2.  We need to associate this vocabulary with a Content type. We have created it specifically for blog entries. So we will, of course, select the **Blog entry** checkbox.

3. For the **Settings**, we declare that the selection of a term from this vocabulary is **Required**, and that the blogger must choose a term from the supplied list.

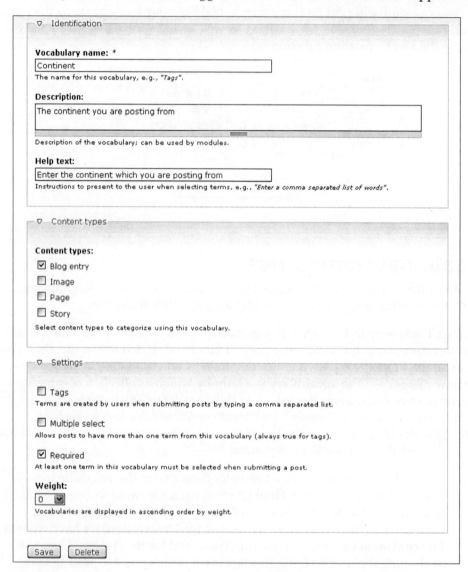

Whereas the vocabulary called **Continent** will have terms included for selection, **Country** and **Location** are free-tagging, meaning that the Hubert will type these in by himself.

| Name | Type | Operations | | |
|------|------|-----------|---|---|
| ✛ Continent | Blog entry | edit vocabulary | list terms | add terms |
| ✛ Country | Blog entry | edit vocabulary | list terms | add terms |
| ✛ Location | Blog entry | edit vocabulary | list terms | add terms |

# Add new terms

Getting back to the **Taxonomy** page, we can see that the new vocabulary that we have just created is now listed. Now we need to add the terms for the **Continent** vocabulary. We do this by clicking on the **add terms** link and then completing the form that we will be presented with. Forget about the **Advanced options** link at the bottom of the page at this stage because we only have a single level of terms.

If you click the **list terms** operation to the righthand side of the vocabulary, then you will be presented with a list of the terms that you have created, in the order that they will be presented to the user. If you don't like this order, then just drag the ones you want to change to the location that you want.

| Terms in *Continent* | List | Add term |

*Continent* is a single hierarchy vocabulary. You may organize the terms in the *Continent* vocabulary by using the handles on the left side of the table. To change the name or description of a term, click the *edit* link next to the term.

[more help...]

| Name | Operations |
|------|-----------|
| ✛ Africa | edit |
| ✛ Antarctica | edit |
| ✛ Asia | edit |
| ✛ Australia | edit |
| ✛ Europe | edit |
| ✛ North America | edit |
| ✛ South America | edit |

[ Save ]  [ Reset to alphabetical ]

# Test the Blog submission form

Now let us test our blog submission form and see how it works. To do this, click on the **Create content** link on the lefthand side of the page, and select **Blog entry**. You will get a form similar to the one shown in following screenshot:

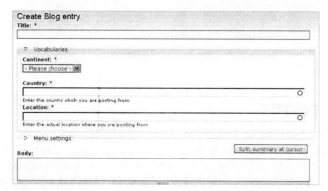

Now add some blog posts to ensure that you have successfully performed the tasks mentioned up to now.

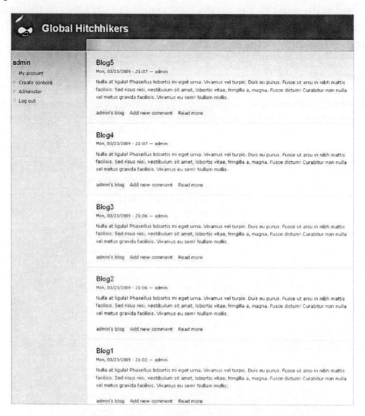

**Tips and traps**

Remember to change the permissions to **create blog entries, create images**, and **upload files** in the **Permissions** page in the **admin** menu.

# Display content

Now, that just about settles much of what is required to post blog posts onto the Global Hitchhikers Club web site. First, we want to be able to view our blog posts by continent.

# Create quick menus with the Taxonomy Menu module

Again there are several ways to do this. One quick method is to use a module known as **Taxonomy Menu**. What this essentially does is permits you to view your blog entries just by clicking on a menu link that corresponds to the title of a vocabulary term.

Download the **Taxonomy Menu** module, and install it. After this, go to the
**Administer** page, and then to the **Taxonomy Menu settings** page. Select the
vocabularies that you want to include in your menu, and save the configuration.
You will now see the links to items related to each vocabulary under the Navigation
menu in the sidebar. If you have posted items into the categories already, then you
will see that your posts appear on the page when you click on the corresponding
menu. If you click on the **Continent | Africa** link, for example, then it will show you
a page containing all blog entries that have been posted to the site from Africa.

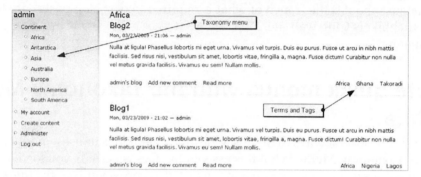

# Quick searching

The **Search** module gives us a form through which the entire site can be searched for
your keyword. Enable this module. Go to the **Blocks** page, and put it in the region
that suits you. In this case, we have located it at the top of the **Left sidebar**. You must
run cron to index the posts before performing a search.

# Menus

Now let's tidy up our site by creating a menu system that is more intuitive. For
simplicity, we will be putting our entire **Continent** page views menu under the
**Primary links** menu, and separating it from our user's menu.

To do this, go to the **Menus** link on the **Administer** page.

1. Click on the **Navigation** link at the top to access the page, which lists all of
   the navigation links.

2. Click on the **edit** link in front of each term, under the vocabulary **Continent**.

3. In the resulting page, change the **Parent Item** to **<Primary links>**, and also
   select the **Expanded** checkbox.

4. After having moved all of the terms under **Continent** to the **Primary links** menu, deselect **Continent** from the **Navigation** link menu.

After saving, you are taken to another page which shows that all of the menu items for the terms have been moved to under the **Primary links** menu.

Now visit the **Blocks** page. Grab the **Primary links** block, and drag it to the **Left sidebar**. On saving the blocks, we will see our new Primary links for Continents neatly placed where they can easily be accessed. While we are on the **Blocks** page, we could also move the **Who's new** and **Who's online** blocks to the **Left sidebar**.

# Finishing up

We may now enable our, **Pushbutton**, theme on the **Themes** page, and configure it to our preferences. We have now given Hubert the hobo a new web site to share his travels with his pals worldwide.

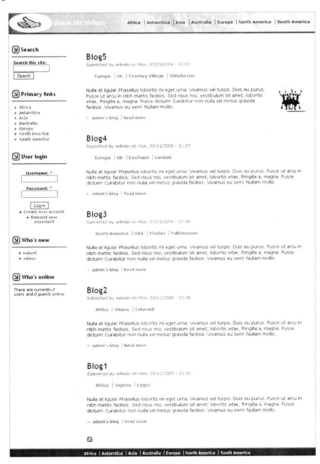

# Summary

In this chapter, you have learned how to:

- Build a basic site for publishing blog posts from multiple users
- Configure the **Profile** module to collect and display user details
- Use free tagging and vocabularies to classify content

# 4

# Breaking Events—Building an Events Site

"Electric" Skid Jackson is a retired break-dancer. Having won the Red Rhino Street Dance Award for five years in a row, Skid is now a full time choreographer and owner of the Def Freeze dance crew. Skid has an idea for a web site where all of the street dance events all over the world can be listed according to their location. The primary advantage of such a web site to Skid will be to provide a constant stream of prize-winning dance duels where he can enter the Def Freeze dance crew. He has chosen the name "Breaking Events" for his web site.

Skid Jackson wants a web site where new events, from anywhere in the world, can be listed on the site by all of the registered users. He also wants to be reminded when any item is posted, so that he can be the first to know what is shaking. Additionally, notifications on new events are sent to all of the site users who have subscribed to receive them.

The Breaking Events web site will have the following features:

- Registered users will be able to create events, categorized by continent
- Calendar—which will show all of the events in a grid view
- A mini calendar in the side bar
- A listing of the latest listed events, shown as teasers, on the front page
- Users can subscribe to receive mail about new postings to the site
- Users can subscribe to be alerted via email when an event draws near

# Theme

The theme chosen for this web site is "Terrafirma", which is a Drupal community contribution. The front page will feature a two-column theme, with the main content accommodating listed events and the sidebar holding the blocks.

# Build the Breaking Events site

To enable this web site to function properly, we need to do the following:

- Create selectable terms for users to describe the Continent in which the event is taking place.
- Establish free tag fields for the user to describe his or her specific location (country and locality). The advantage of free tagging is that the users can be quite precise when describing their positions.
- Select the modules necessary to implement the required functionalities and configure them.
- Categorize and organize all of the content in a logical way in order to enable them to be easily accessed and read.

# Modules

From the tasks that are required by this project, we are able to build a list of contributed modules that will be used. The "Breaking Events" web site is built entirely around the **Event** module, and should be fairly easy to build.

# Optional Core modules

For the purpose of our example, we shall be using the following **Core** modules:

- **Taxonomy** — enables us to classify our content
- **Comment** — permits users to comment on stories
- **Upload** — allows the upload of files and images into content
- **Search** — enables site-wide searching by keyword

# Contributed modules

For the purpose of this example, we shall be using the following contributed modules:

- **Event** — allows the creation of event-type content.
- **Notify** — allows users and admin to receive periodic emails about all the new or revised content and / or comments.
- **Signup** — allows users to sign up for content of any type.
- **Image** — allows users with the correct permissions to upload images. Thumbnails and additional sizes are created automatically.

- **IMCE** — gives the client the ability to upload and manage some files through the Admin interface.

- **Taxonomy Menu** — easily transforms taxonomy vocabularies into menus.

- **Tiny MCE** — makes adding page breaks and setting drop caps in the articles a bit easier.

- **Poormanscron** — runs the Drupal cron operations without needing the cron application.

## Enable modules

First, visit the modules page and enable all of the modules that we need. For simplicity, just select all of the checkboxes related to the modules that we have listed.

# Basic content

The site is built around the **Event** module, which automatically creates its own content type. However, the main challenges that we will still be presented with are:

- How to categorize the content in a way that will make it easy to find

- How to create the alert system for newly-listed events

- How to create the alert system for upcoming events

# Configure the Events module

We must configure the **Events** module before it can function. In order to do this, visit the link for the **Events** module on the **Administer** page. The page will have a section similar to the following screenshot:

Events

Event overview
Change how event summary information is displayed.

Timezone handling
Change how timezone information is saved and displayed.

# Event overview

Go to the **Event overview** setting page. This is where you will set values like how many items are listed in the upcoming event block that the module will provide on the **Blocks** page, as well as overviews and controls. Leave these settings with their default values, or change them to the appropriate values, as per your needs.

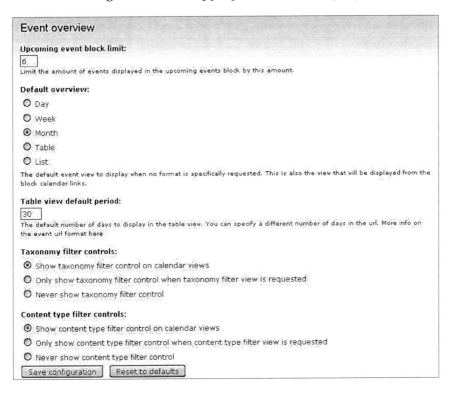

# Time zone handling

We can leave the time zone settings at the default settings for now. Later on, you will be prompted to enter the time zones for the events.

# Date and time

Visit the **Date and time** link on the **Administer** page, and set it to the time zone that you want to adopt for your site, and select how you want dates to be formatted.

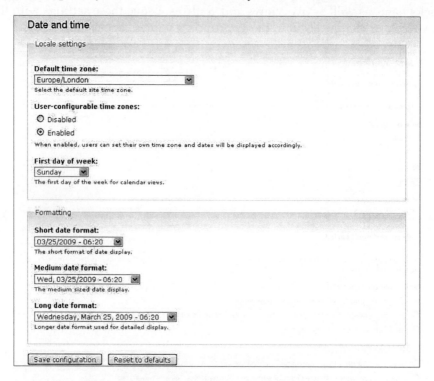

# Configure the Notification module

Skid Jackson desires that his site users should be able to receive notifications for newly-listed events, so that they are kept abreast of the news on up-coming events.

Visit the **Notification settings** link on the **Administer** page. Here, you will be presented with a page that will enable you to set how often you want notifications to be sent, as well as for which kind of Content type notification may be sent.

1. We want the notification to be sent every week, so we select the **1 week** option.

2. The notification should be sent for the **Event** Content type, so we select the **Event** checkbox.

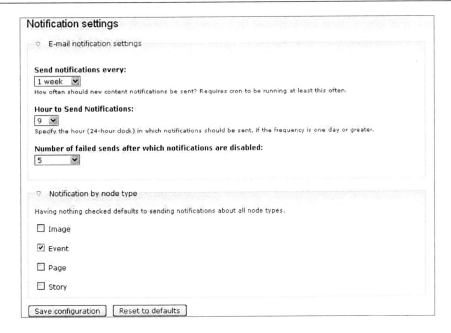

## Configure the Event Content type

Ensure that you have enabled the **Event** module. By navigating to the **Administer** page of the site and then into the **Content management** section, we will find the **Content types** link.

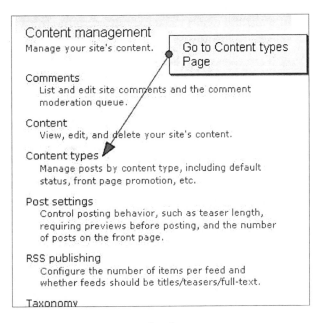

If we access this page, then we will see the various Content types listed there. We will not be creating any new Content type.

| Name | Type | Description | Operations |
|------|------|-------------|------------|
| Event | event | Events have a start date and an optional end date as well as a teaser and a body. They can be extended by other modules, too. | edit  delete |
| Image | image | An image (with thumbnail). This is ideal for publishing photographs or screenshots. | edit |
| Page | page | A *page*, similar in form to a *story*, is a simple method for creating and displaying information that rarely changes, such as an "About us" section of a website. By default, a *page* entry does not allow visitor comments and is not featured on the site's initial home page. | edit  delete |
| Story | story | A *story*, similar in form to a *page*, is ideal for creating and displaying content that informs or engages website visitors. Press releases, site announcements, and informal blog-like entries may all be created with a *story* entry. By default, a *story* entry is automatically featured on the site's initial home page, and provides the ability to post comments. | edit  delete |

1.  Click on the **edit** link of the **Event** Content type. You will then be presented with a form.

2.  In the **Workflow setting**, we need to determine the default options:
    - Do you want the event to be published and available for use on the site, immediately after submission? If so, select the **Published** checkbox.
    - Do you want the event to be promoted to the front page? If so, select the **Promoted to front page** checkbox.
    - Do you want the event to remain at the top of the list of contents on the site? If so, select the **Sticky at top of list** checkbox. For this project we should avoid this option.

3.  In the **Comments settings** panel, you can indicate whether you want to allow comments to be made on events or not, and if you do, then how these comments will be handled.

4.  In the **Signup settings** panel, select the **Enabled (on by default)** option.

5.  In the **Event calendar** setting, select the **All Views** option.

# Images

At the bottom of the form for this Content type, you will see a panel for **Image Attach settings**. Enable **Attach images**, and now your **Event** Content type will be ready to incorporate images. To confirm this, go to the **Create content** link again for the **Event** Content type. Near the bottom of the page, you will find the **Attached images** panel where you can upload images for your events.

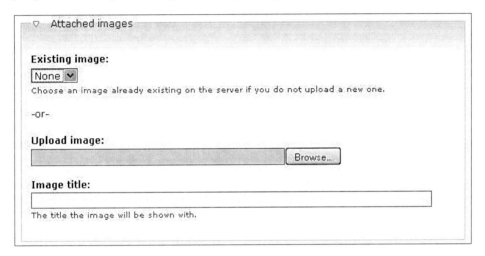

If you have also configured your TinyMCE editor correctly, then you should have an editor bar, which is similar to the one shown in the following screenshot in the **Body** field. You can similarly post images into the body of your **Event** by using the upload image function in TinyMCE.

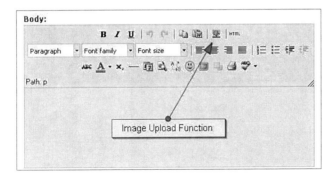

# Create new categories

Our events will be organized into categories in order to group them together with other events according to geographical location.

Go to the **Taxonomy** link under the **Content management** section on the **Administer** page, and navigate to the **Taxonomy** page. If you have started a new site, then you will see at the foot of this page a notice that there is no vocabulary available for your new categories. The **vocabulary** is a term by which a collection of categories (or terms) can be collectively described. In this case, let us create three vocabularies — Continent, Country, and Location. We will do this by clicking on the **Add vocabulary** link at the top of the page. This is what we will be filling into the form for this new vocabulary.

1.  In the **Identification** panel, let us enter the name of the vocabulary, a **Description**, as well as any **Help text** that comes to mind to guide the users when they come across this vocabulary. For the Continent, we have used **Continent** as the **Vocabulary name**. For the **Description**, we have entered **The continent you are posting from**. For the **Help text**, we will be instructing the user to **Enter the continent which you are posting from**.

2.  We need to associate this vocabulary with a Content type. We have created it specifically for **Event**, so we will naturally select the **Event** checkbox.

3.  For the settings, we declare that the selection of a term from this vocabulary is **Required**, and the person posting the content must choose a term from the supplied list.

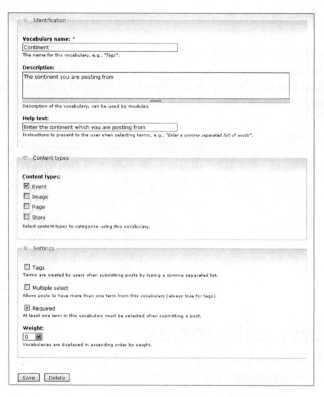

Whereas the vocabulary called **Continent** will have terms included for selection, **Country** and **Location** are free-tagging, meaning that the person posting the content must type these in.

| Name | Type | Operations | | |
|------|------|-----------|---|---|
| ⊹ Continent | Blog entry | edit vocabulary | list terms | add terms |
| ⊹ Country | Blog entry | edit vocabulary | list terms | add terms |
| ⊹ Location | Blog entry | edit vocabulary | list terms | add terms |

On returning to the **Taxonomy** page, we see that the new vocabulary that we have just created has been listed. Now we need to add the terms for the **Continent** vocabulary. We do this by clicking on the **add terms** link, and completing the form that we will be presented with. Forget the **Advanced options** link at the bottom of the page at this stage, because we only have a single level of terms.

If you click on the **list terms** link on the vocabulary, then you will be presented with a list of the terms that you have created, in the order that they will be presented to the user. If you don't like this order, then just drag the ones you want to change to the location that you want.

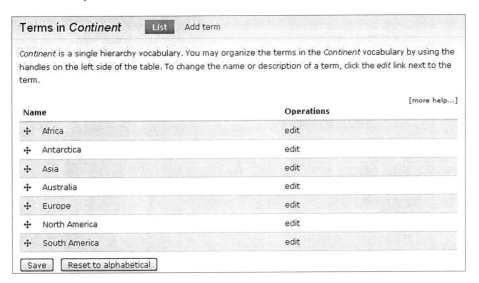

# Test the Event submission form

Now let us test our Event submission form, and see how it works. To do this, click on the **Create content** link on the lefthand side menu, and select **Event**. You will get a form, similar to the one shown in the following screenshot:

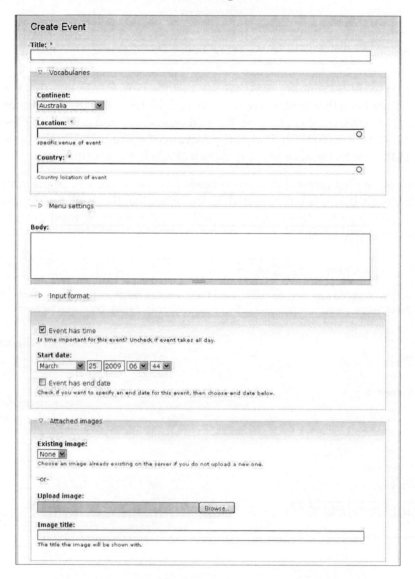

Post some events, to make sure that the site has been correctly set up, and make sure that the posts are promoted to the front page. You should end up with a front page similar to the one shown in the following screenshot:

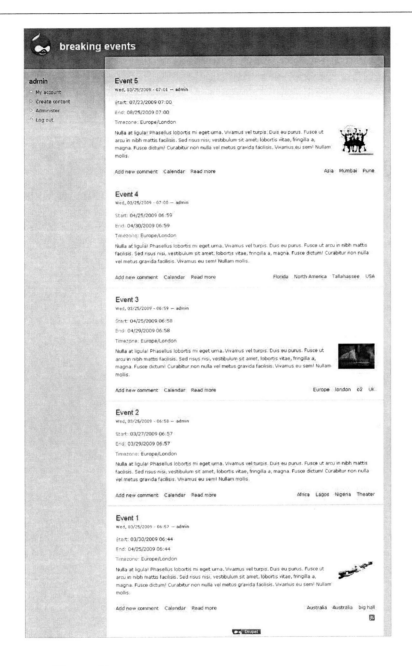

> **Tips and traps**
>
>
>
> Remember to change the permissions to **create event content**, **create images**, and **upload file** on the **Permissions** page.
>
> Without enabling the **Poormanscron** module, the notification will not work.

# Display content

The **Taxonomy Menu** module will permit you to view your events just by clicking on a menu link that corresponds to the title of a vocabulary term. We want to be able to view our events by Continent.

# Create quick menus with the Taxonomy Menu module

Download the **Taxonomy Menu** module, and install it. After this, go to the **Administer** page, and then to the **Taxonomy Menu settings** page. Select the vocabularies that you want to include in your menu, and save the configuration. You will now see the links to items related to each vocabulary under the Navigation menu in the sidebar.

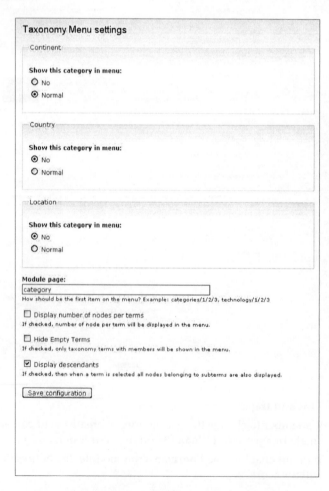

If you have posted items into the categories already, then you will see that your posts appear on the page when we click on the corresponding menu. For example, if you click on the **Continent | Asia** link, then you will see a page containing the events that have taken place, or will take place, in **Asia**.

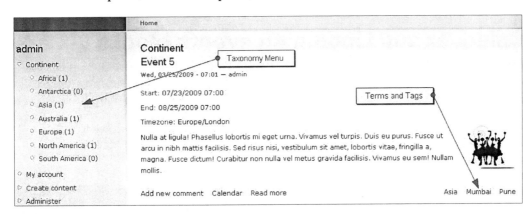

# Menus

Now let's tidy up our site by creating a menu system that is more intuitive. For simplicity, we will be keeping our entire Continent page views menu separate from our user's menu. We will be putting them all under the **Primary links** menu.

To do this, go to the **Menu** link on the **Administer** page.

1. Click on the **Navigation** link at the top to access the **Navigation** page, which lists all of the navigation links.
2. Click on the **edit** link in front of each term under the vocabulary **Continent**.
3. In the resulting page, change the **Parent Item** to **<Primary links>**, and also select the **Expanded** checkbox.
4. After having moved all of the terms under **Continent** to the **Primary links** menu, deselect **Continent** from the **Navigation** link menu.

After saving, you are taken to another page which shows that all of the menu items for the terms have been moved under **Primary links** menu.

Now visit the **Blocks** page, grab the **Primary links** block, and drag it to the **Right sidebar**. After saving the blocks, you will see your new **Primary links** block for the Continents neatly placed on the lefthand side of the page, from where they can easily be accessed.

# Calendar and Upcoming events blocks

There is a calendar view block provided by the **Event** module. In order to make this easily accessible, we will place it on the sidebar. There is also an upcoming events block listing the nearest events, which we will also place on the sidebar.

Go to the **Blocks** link on the **admin** menu, and move these two modules to the **Right sidebar**. If we return to the front page, we will then have the blocks arranged, as shown in the following screenshot:

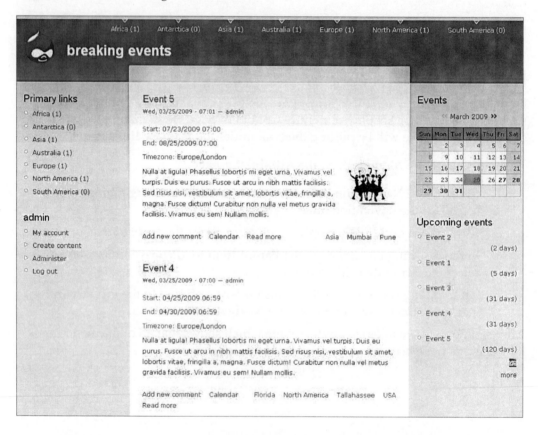

On clicking the month link at the top of the calendar, we are presented with the following page view, which allows a more detailed view of individual events:

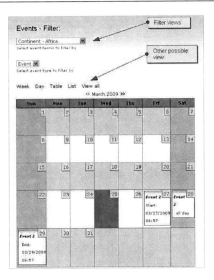

There, if you click on any event panel, you will see a page similar to following screenshot, showing the details of the event. It also shows a link at the bottom, through which qualified users may sign up to participate in the event.

# Finishing up

We may now enable our new, **Terrafirma**, theme on the **Themes** page, and configure it according to our preferences.

# Summary

In this chapter, you have learned how to:

- Build a basic site for listing events from multiple users
- Use the **Notify** module to enable a user to get notifications of new content posted
- Make use of free-tagging to classify content

# 5

# Drupbook—Building a Community Site

Tony Tortilla is a student at Drupelburg University. Tony thinks that the social life could be vastly improved if the University had its own community web site where the students could get to know each other a little better. With about 5,000 students, Tony thinks that the idea might immediately make him a big hit with the chicks, and also possibly make him lots of money in the future, when the site is bought by Google. So, Tony Tortilla has come up with the idea of Drupbook—a simple community web site for the students at Drupelburg University.

Drupbook is intended to be quite simple initially, and will have the following main features:

- Users will be able to create detailed profile pages for themselves (names , interests, and so on)
- Users will be able to create blogs, which will be shown on a general blog page and be available for comments
- Users will be able to create special interest groups of their own
- There will be a forum for users to express their views and opinions on several subjects including books, music, film and video, and concerts
- Users will be able to create polls and have others vote on them
- Users will have access to real-time chat

# Theme

The theme chosen is "Multiflex-3", which is a contribution theme. Tony chose this theme as he liked it and thought it would attract interest and draw favorable attention from the University students.

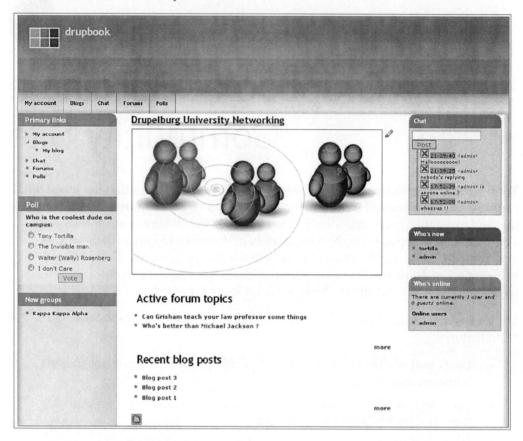

# Build Drupbook

Tony is not looking for anything fancy like **Facebook** or **MySpace** but just a weekend project. All he wants is a simple community portal with basic social networking features, which can be summarized as follows:

- Tony wants users to be able to create and maintain clubs on the portal
- He wants users to be able to share their interests, knowledge, and opinions on several social topics
- He needs users to be able to hold online conversations in real time, in live chat

In order to create this site, we need to do the following:

- Establish profile pages where users may fully describe themselves. Profile pages will contain name, email, mobile phone number, age, gender, faculty, and so on.
- Select the modules necessary to implement the required functionalities, and configure them.
- Create blogging functionality to enable users to share their journals with one another.
- Create a forum for discussing entertainment topics and, principally, books, music, film & video, and concerts.
- Enable users to create polls.
- Enable users to chat with one another in real time.
- Enable users to create clubs and invite other members to join.
- Organize all of the content in a logical way in order to enable it to be easily accessed and read.

# Modules

For Tony Tortilla's community web site, we shall be using the following modules:

# Optional Core modules

The Optional Core modules are included in the basic Drupal installation, and these will have to be enabled:

- **Taxonomy**—enables us to classify our content
- **Comment**—allows users to comment on stories
- **Upload**—allows the upload of files and images into content
- **Profile**—allows the configuration of user profiles
- **Forum**—enables threaded discussions about general topics
- **Poll**—allows your site to capture votes on different topics in the form of multiple choice questions
- **Blog**—enables user web pages or blogs to be updated easily and regularly
- **Search**—enables site-wide searching by keyword

# Contributed modules

The following Contributed modules will need to be obtained from the Drupal web site, uploaded, and enabled:

- **OG** – enables users to create and manage their own 'groups'
- **Tribune** – provides an advanced discussion space, such as a chat room
- **Image** – allows users with the correct permissions to upload images (thumbnails and additional sizes of images are created automatically)
- **IMCE** – gives the client the ability to upload and manage files through the Admin interface

# Basic content

The site is built around several modules that give it the "community" functionality. In this case, the main challenge will be to make the features enabled by these modules to be easily accessible and to be harmonized. Tony will also want the users to have a standard profile form so that uniformity (of the information that they present to other users) can be maintained. This will enable other users to know what they should expect to find on a user profile. It will also enable structured searches of profiles.

# User settings

The basic user settings may be found as a link on the **Administer** page, and the page that it opens to is called the **User settings** page. At the bottom of this page, we will enable **Signature support.** We will also enable **Picture support** so that the users can have their pictures shown on their profiles.

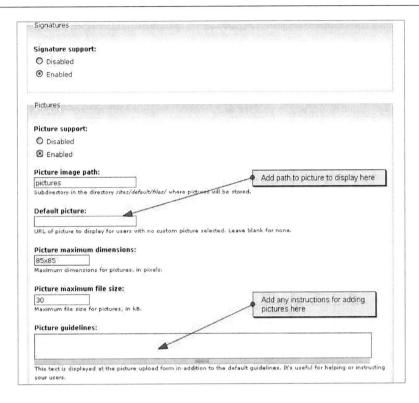

To get the desired user profile page, we need to enable the **Profile** module
on the **Modules** page. On visiting the **Profiles** link on the **Administer** page,
we will be presented with a page similar to the one shown in following screenshot:

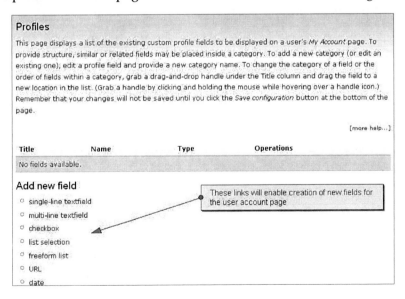

- User's name [textfield]
- Alternative Email [textfield]
- Mobile phone number [textfield]
- Date of birth [date]
- Gender [list selection]
- Faculty [list selection]
- Blab about me [textarea]

# Name

The **Name** field is a **single-line textfield**. So this is the link that we will click on to create this field.

- In the **Category** field, let us enter **Personal Information** because that is exactly what this is all about
- For the **Title**, enter **Name**
- For the **Form name**, enter **profile_name**
- For **Visibility**, select **Public field, content shown on profile page but not used on member list pages**
- For the **Page title**, enter **People whose name is %value**
- Select all of the last three checkboxes to make this field compulsory, auto-completed, and visible when users are newly registering

The completed **Name** field form is shown in the following screenshot:

**Field settings**

**Category:** *
Personal Information ○
The category the new field should be part of. Categories are used to group fields logically. An example category is "Personal information".

**Title:** *
Name
The title of the new field. The title will be shown to the user. An example title is "Favorite color".

**Form name:** *
profile_name
The name of the field. The form name is not shown to the user but used internally in the HTML code and URLs. Unless you know what you are doing, it is highly recommended that you prefix the form name with profile_ to avoid name clashes with other fields. Spaces or any other special characters except dash (-) and underscore (_) are not allowed. An example name is "profile_favorite_color" or perhaps just "profile_color".

**Explanation:**
Enter your name

An optional explanation to go with the new field. The explanation will be shown to the user.

**Visibility:**

○ Hidden profile field, only accessible by administrators, modules and themes.

○ Private field, content only available to privileged users.

◉ Public field, content shown on profile page but not used on member list pages.

○ Public field, content shown on profile page and on member list pages.

**Page title:**
People whose favorite name is %value"
To enable browsing this field by value, enter a title for the resulting page. The word %value will be substituted with the corresponding value. An example page title is "People whose favorite color is %value". This is only applicable for a public field.

**Weight:**
-10 ▾
The weights define the order in which the form fields are shown. Lighter fields "float up" towards the top of the category.

☑ Form will auto-complete while user is typing.
For security, auto-complete will be disabled if the user does not have access to user profiles.

☑ The user must enter a value.

☑ Visible in user registration form.

The **Alternative Email** and **Mobile Phone Number** fields are created using a similar procedure.

# Date of Birth

The **Date of Birth** field is a **date** field. So we will click on the **date** link to create this field.

- In the **Category** field, let us enter **Personal Information**, because that is exactly what this is all about
- For the **Title**, enter **Date of Birth**
- For the **Form name**, enter **profile_dob**
- For **Visibility**, select **Public field, content shown on profile page but not used on member list pages**
- Select all of the last three checkboxes to make this field compulsory, auto-completed, and visible when users are newly registering

# Gender

This is a **list selection** field because each user is either male, or female; we'll add the "I don't know" category for political correctness. Select the **list selection** link.

- In the **Category** field, let us enter **Personal Information**
- For the **Title**, enter **Gender**
- For the **Form name**, enter **profile_gender**
- For **Selection options**, enter **Male, Female** and **I don't know** on separate lines
- For **Visibility**, select **Public field, content shown on profile page but not used on member list pages**
- For the **Page title**, enter **People whose gender is %value**
- Select all of the last three checkboxes to make this field compulsory, auto-completed, and visible when users are newly registering

# Faculty

This is also a **list selection** field, as each user will only belong to one faculty at a time. Drupelburg University has only four faculties—Arts, Engineering, Science, and Medicine. Select the **list selection** link.

- In the **Category** field, let us enter **Personal Information**
- For the **Title**, enter **Faculty**
- For the **Form name**, enter **profile_faculty**
- For **Selection options**, enter **Arts**, **Engineering**, **Science**, and **Medicine** on separate lines
- For **Visibility**, select **Public field, content shown on profile page but not used on member list pages**
- For the **Page title**, enter **People whose faculty is %value**
- Select all of the last three checkboxes to make this field compulsory, auto-completed, and visible when users are newly registering

# About Me

The **About Me** field is a **multi-line textfield**. This is the link that we will click on to create this field.

- In the **Category** field, let us enter **Personal Information**
- For the **Title**, enter **About Me**
- For the **Form name**, enter **profile_about**
- For **Visibility**, select **Public field, content shown on profile page but not used on member list pages**
- Select all of the last three checkboxes to make this field compulsory, auto-completed, and visible when users are newly registering

The completed **About Me** field form is shown in the following screenshot:

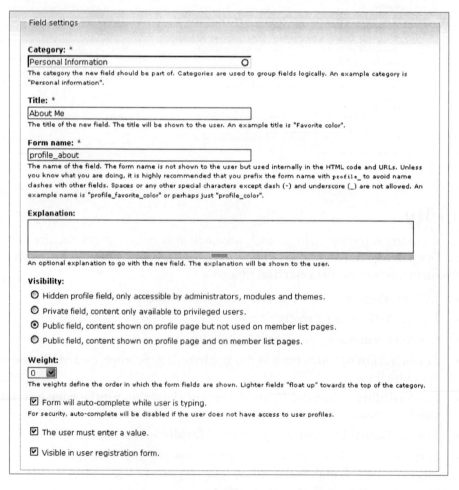

Once all of the fields have been created, our new profile creation page looks similar to the one shown in following screenshot:

| Title | Name | Type | Operations |
|---|---|---|---|
| **Personal Information** | | | |
| ✛ Name | profile_name | textfield | edit delete |
| ✛ Alternative Email | profile_email | textfield | edit delete |
| ✛ Mobile Phone Number | profile_phone | textfield | edit delete |
| ✛ Date of Birth | profile_dob | date | edit delete |
| ✛ Gender | profile_gender | selection | edit delete |
| ✛ Faculty | profile_faculty | selection | edit delete |
| ✛ About Me | profile_about | textarea | edit delete |

Save the configuration. Note that we have elected to have all of these fields show on the user registration page. To make sure that this works the way we planned it, let's log out from admin for a minute, and attempt to register as a new user by going to the **Create New Account** link. The new user registration form that we created is shown in the following screenshot:

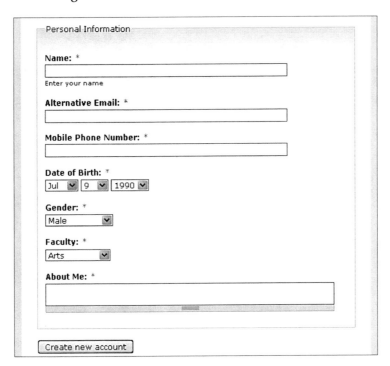

So our profile page is properly configured the way we want it, and the following screenshot summarizes what happens when Tony Tortilla completes his profile:

# Configure the Blog entry Content type

The **Blog entry** Content type is automatically created when the core **Blog** module is enabled. This Content type will permit users to post blog posts that are simply user journals. Ensure that you have enabled the **Blog** module.

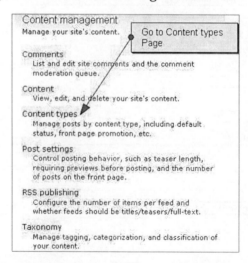

By browsing onto the **Administer** page of the site and then into the **Content management** section, we will find the **Content types** link. If we access this page, then we will see the various Content types listed there. We will not be creating a new Content type as the **Blog entry** Content type is already present, as shown in the following screenshot:

| Content types | List | Add content type | | |
|---|---|---|---|---|

Below is a list of all the content types on your site. All posts that exist on your site are instances of one of these content types.

| Name | Type | Description | Operations | |
|---|---|---|---|---|
| Blog entry | blog | A *blog entry* is a single post to an online journal, or *blog*. | edit | |
| Page | page | A *page*, similar in form to a *story*, is a simple method for creating and displaying information that rarely changes, such as an "About us" section of a website. By default, a *page* entry does not allow visitor comments and is not featured on the site's initial home page. | edit | delete |
| Story | story | A *story*, similar in form to a *page*, is ideal for creating and displaying content that informs or engages website visitors. Press releases, site announcements, and informal blog-like entries may all be created with a *story* entry. By default, a *story* entry is automatically featured on the site's initial home page, and provides the ability to post comments. | edit | delete |

1. Click on the **Blog entry** Content type's **edit** link. You will then be presented with a form.

2. In the **Workflow setting** panel, we need to determine the following options:

   ○ Do you want the blog entry to be published and made available for use on the site immediately after submission? If so, select the **Published** checkbox.

   ○ Do you want the blog entry to be promoted to the front page? If so, select the **Promoted to front page** checkbox.

   ○ Do you want the blog entry to remain at the top of the list of contents on the site? If so, select the **Sticky at top of list** checkbox. In our example, we do not want to make the content sticky.

3. In the **Comments settings** section, you can indicate whether you want to allow comments to be made on blog entries or not, and if you do, then how these comments will be handled.

# Images

You can see that the submission forms for blog posts and other Content types have no place to enable us to add images. Download the **IMCE**, and **Image** modules, and install and enable them. Finally, you must also enable the **Upload** module, or else users will not be able to attach images and other files to their posts.

Having done this, return to **Administer | Content management | Content types,** and check all of the Content type pages again. At the bottom of the Content type's page, you will see a new panel for **Image Attach settings**. Enable **Attach images,** and now your content will be ready to incorporate images. To confirm this, go to the **Create content** link again for the **Blog entry** Content type. Near the bottom of the page, you will find the **Attached images** panel where users can upload images for their blog entries.

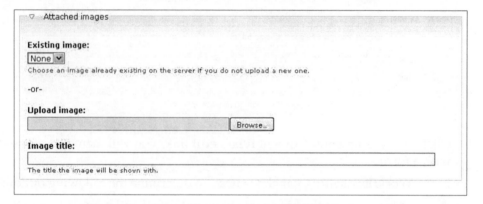

# Test the Blog submission form

Now let us test our blog entry submission form, and see how it works. In order to do this, click on the **Create content** link on the left, and select **Blog entry**. You will get a form similar to the one shown in the following screenshot:

Now add some blog posts to ensure that you have done everything correctly.

# Configure Polls

Now let's configure the polls. If you have not enabled the **Poll** module in your **Modules** page, then go and do so now. When you return to the **Content types** page, you will see that a **Poll** Content type has been automatically created, and the text alongside it describes what a poll is, for you:

> *"A poll is a question with a set of possible responses. A poll, once created, automatically provides a simple running count of the number of votes received for each response."*

The poll is for obtaining feedback on various topics from users.

Let us create a sample poll for the users of Tony Tortilla's Drupbook. Our poll will be like this:

Who is the coolest dude on campus?

- Tony Tortilla
- The Invisible man
- Walter (Wally) Rosenberg
- I don't Care

To create this poll, go to the **Create content** link, and then select **Poll**. Enter your question, the selections, the value that you want to award to each selection, and the duration of your poll. We have given all of the options the same value ("**1**" in this example).

On saving the poll, you should get a polling form similar to the one shown in the following screenshot:

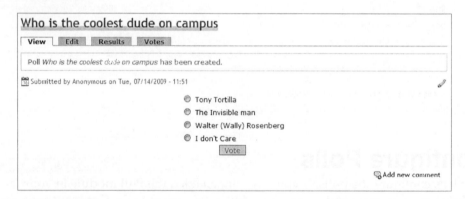

But we don't really want to see the poll as a page view; we want it in the sidebar. If we make a quick visit to the **Blocks** page, then we will find that a block for the **Most recent poll** has been created. Now move this block to the **Left sidebar**, and save the setting. After you've done this, you will see the latest poll block on the left (where we want it).

# Configure Forums

Creating the forums should also be easy. Go to the **Modules** page, and enable the **Forum** module. On the **Forums** page in **Administer | Content management**, you will be presented with a blank page. Here, we will create a single "Container" that has four forum boards for **Books**, **Music**, **Film & Video**, and **Concerts**. Let's call the container **General Topics**.

In order to do this, look for the links at the top of the page, and follow the instructions for creating the container and for creating the forum. Each of the forum boards (**Books, Music, Film & Video,** and **Concerts**) will have the container **General Topics** as a parent.

| Name | Operations |
|---|---|
| ✥ General Topics | edit container |
| ✥ Books | edit forum |
| ✥ Concerts | edit forum |
| ✥ Film & Video | edit forum |
| ✥ Music | edit forum |

Posting to the forum requires that you follow the process that you must have become quite familiar with by now. Go to the **Create content** link, and look for the **Forum topic** Content type. You will be presented with a form similar to those you have seen already. When you have completed this form, you will have created a forum topic. While at it, add a few more topics.

# Configure Chat

There are several other modules capable of adding the chat functionality to the community web site, but the **Tribune** module has been selected, just as an example and not because it is better than any other. Go to the **Modules** page in **Administer | Site building,** and enable the **Tribune** module. Then return to the **Administer** page, and look for the **Tribune** link, which will lead to a configuration page. Most of the settings in this page may safely be left with their default values.

If you click on the **Tribune** link on the **Left sidebar,** then it will lead you to the users chat page.

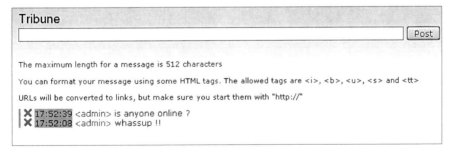

Now let us go to the **Blocks** page, and move the **Tribune** block to the **Right sidebar** to make this feature more easily accessible. Rename the block to **Chat** to make it look more familiar to users.

# Configure Organic groups

Organic groups will enable users to set up groups or clubs of their own, and invite others to participate. Go to the **Modules** page, and enable OG modules—specifically the **Organic group access control** module.

After returning to the **Administer** page, we should look for the **Organic groups configuration** link, which will present us with a settings page.

At the top of this new page, you will initially see an error message asking you to define your **Group nodes** and **Standard group post** Content types.

# Create new Group Content type

By navigating to the **Administer** page of the site and then into the **Content** management section, we will find the **Content types** link. If we access this page, then we will see the various content types listed there.

1.  Click on the **Add content type** link at the top; you will then be presented with a form.

2.  Add the Content type's descriptions, the general rules for the adding of content to, and displaying of content from, this new Content type, in the places where they need to be in the form.

3.  In the **Identification** fields, add a **Name** and **Description** for the Content type.

4.  In the **Submission form settings**, you can choose the title that you want to give the fields. By default, you are presented with **Title** (for the title of the submission), **Body** (for the main story), and also the fields demanding the minimum length an article must be before it can be accepted for submission, as well as another place where you can describe submission guidelines for this Content type.

5.  In the **Workflow settings**, we need to determine the default options. Do you want the article to be published and made available for use on the site, immediately after submission? Do you want it promoted to the front page? Do you want it to remain at the top of the list of contents on the site? If the answer is "No" to any off these questions, then ignore the relevant option.

6.  In the **Comments settings**, indicate whether you want to allow comments to be made for articles from this Content type or not, and if you do, then how these comments will be handled.

Now return again to the Organic groups configuration page. **Edit** the presented Content types, and set **Story** as **Standard group post** and **Group** as **Group node**. You may, at this point, leave other settings with their default values. The following screenshot gives us a visual cue of what has to be done:

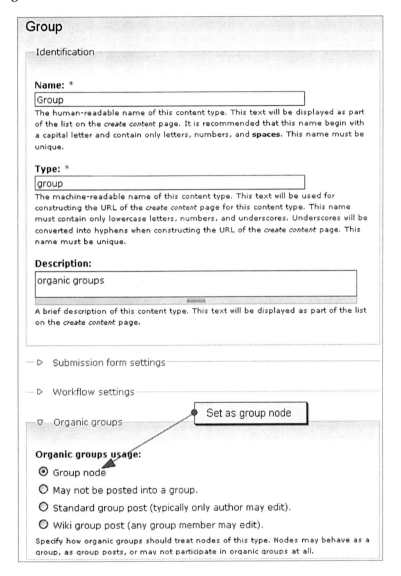

# Create a Group

We have designated the **Group** Content type as our group node, which means that it is the Content type that will always be used to create groups. Therefore, in order to create a new group, we go to the **Create content** link, and then select **Group**. This will present a page as shown in the following screenshot:

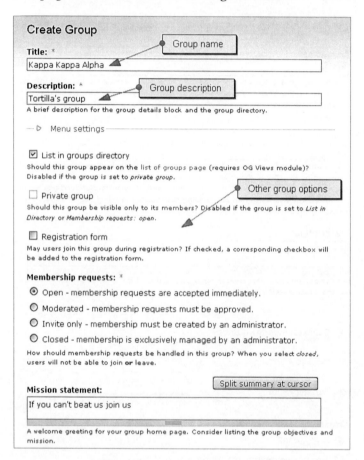

We define the name of the group and its visibility on this page. After we have created the new group, we may go to the **Blocks** page, and move the **New groups** block to the **Left sidebar**, It should show the details of the group there to all of the users who have access privileges to the group.

# Put it all together

Now we need to tie all of the elements of the project together to make the site more meaningful to the users.

# Front page

From our design, we need to move the latest blog posts and active forum topics to the front page. We can easily do this on the **Blocks** page. Move the required blocks to the **Content** region, and configure them to show only on the front page.

Also move the **Who's online** and **Who's new** blocks to the sidebar, where we want them.

# Menus

Now let's tidy up our site by creating a menu system that is more intuitive. For simplicity, we will be putting our links to **My account**, **Blogs**, **Chat**, **Forums**, **Polls** menu all under the **Primary links** menu, and separate from our navigation menu.

In order to do this, go to the **Menu** link on the **Administer** page, and select **Site building**.

- Click on the **Navigation** link at the top to access the page that lists all of the navigation links
- Click on the **Edit** link in front of **My account**
- In the resulting page, change the **Parent Item** to **<Primary links>** and also select **Expanded**

After saving, you are taken to another page showing that all of the menu items for the terms have been moved under the **Primary links** menu. Do this for the remaining menus — **Blogs**, **Chat**, **Forums**, and **Polls**.

Now visit the **Blocks** page, grab the **Primary links** block, and drag it to the **Left sidebar** from where all of the features can now easily be accessed.

**Tips and traps**

You must remember to visit the **Permissions** page on the **Administer | User management** to control what site users are permitted to do. Basically, they should be permitted full access to blogs, forums, images, comments, polls, chat, and user relationship.

# Finishing up

We may now enable our new theme, **Multiflex-3**, on the **Themes** page. Tony Tortilla now has a new social networking site for his friends and the entire Drupelburg University student community!

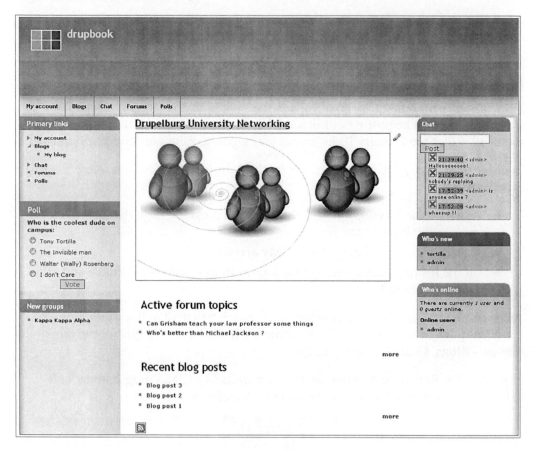

# Summary

In this chapter, you have learned how to:

- Build a basic web site for social networking
- Configure the **Forums, Polls, Organic groups, Chat,** and so on as community features for the portal

# The Daily Drupe–Building a Newspaper Site

The Daily Drupe is the only newspaper in Drupelburg, and it has a local circulation. The newspaper carries a variety of articles organized into several categories:

**NEWS**

- Local
- World
- Business

**SPORTS**

- Football
- Cricket
- Golf
- Snooker

**OPINION**

- Editorial
- Letters

**FEATURES**

- Politics
- Arts
- Media
- Science
- Natural Health
- Law
- Education
- Fashion
- Food & Drink
- Auto

The intention is to replicate the content of The Daily Drupe — online — in a way that will enable the online edition to be easily updated on a real-time basis. Typically, stories will be posted from all over Drupelburg to be approved by the Editor before they are promoted to be read.

In addition to the usual stories, it has been decided by the publisher to introduce some other community features that will encourage users to visit the web site more often. So The Daily Drupe will also include a forum — for readers to join discussions on various topics.

# Theme

The theme chosen is "Analytic", which is a Drupal community contribution. The front page will feature a three-column theme, with the content area in the middle, which is further arranged into panels to accommodate blocks of content.

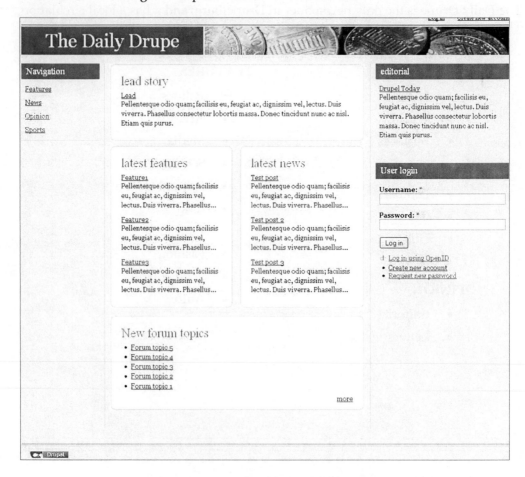

# Build The Daily Drupe online

The primary challenges of this project will be how to:

- Normalize, categorize, and organize all of the content in a logical way in order to enable it to be easily accessed and read

- Select the modules necessary to implement the required functionalities, and to configure them

- Implement the front page design without altering the templates of the core theme that we will be using

# Modules

From the tasks that are presented by this project, we are able to build a list of contributed modules that will be used. There are often several ways of getting the same result, with each method undoubtedly requiring different combinations of contributed and Core modules, but for the purpose of this example we shall be using the following modules:

# Optional Core modules

We will be using the following **Core** modules, which are enabled from the **Modules** page:

- **Taxonomy** — enables us to classify our content
- **Comment** — permits users to comment on stories
- **Upload** — allows the upload of files and images into content

# Contributed modules

We will also be using the following contributed modules, which are uploaded and then enabled from the **Modules** page:

- **Image** — allows users with the correct permissions to upload images. Thumbnails and additional sizes of images are created automatically.

- **IMCE** — gives the client ability to upload and manage some files through the Admin interface.

- **Panels** — this module allows you to create pages that are divided into areas of the page.

- **Taxonomy Menu** — easily transforms any of your taxonomy vocabularies into menus.
- **Tiny MCE** — makes adding page breaks and setting drop caps in the articles a bit easier.
- **Views** — provides a flexible method of controlling how lists of content are presented.

# Categorize content

What we need to do first is to establish how the content is going to be organized for use on the site. Having an existing print-based publication has made it easier for us to establish the relationship between the various Content types. For example, News as a Content type has categories for Local, World, and Business news. So, there is no need to create Local News as a main Content type, but it can be created as a News category. We will establish Sports as a major Content type, with Football, Cricket, Golf, and Snooker as categories. We shall do the same for all the other listed content.

| NEWS | SPORTS | OPINION | FEATURES |
|---|---|---|---|
| Local | Football | Editorial | Politics |
| World | Cricket | Letters | Arts |
| Business | Golf | | Media |
| | Snooker | | Science |
| | | | Natural Health |
| | | | Law |
| | | | Education |
| | | | Fashion |
| | | | Food & Drink |
| | | | Auto |

We have now defined the framework for how content will be organized on the site. Now let us implement these rules.

# Create new Content types

By going to the **Administer** page of the site and then to the **Content management** section, we will find the **Content types** link.

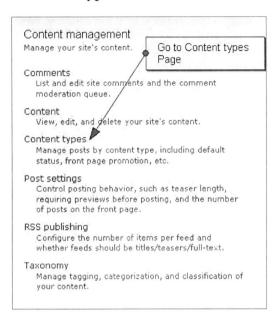

If we access this page, then we will see the various Content types listed there. Our needs are not so basic, so we will need to create our own new **Content types** for News, Sports, Features, and Opinion.

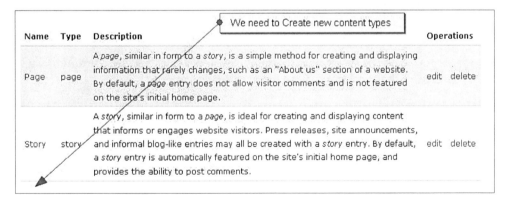

To do this, we will go by the following procedure:

1. Click on the **Add content type** link at the top. You will then be presented with a form.

2. Add the Content type descriptions and the general rules for the adding of content to, and display of content from this new content type, in the places where they need to be on the form. Here are some guides:

   a. In the **Identification** fields, add the **Name** and **Description** of the Content type.

   b. In the **Submission Form settings**, choose the title that you want to give the fields. By default, you are presented with **Title** (for the title of the submission), **Body** (for the main story), and also fields defining the minimum length of an article before it can be accepted for submission, as well as another place where you can describe submission guidelines for this Content type. Leave this at the system default setting.

   c. In the **Workflow setting,** we need to determine the default options:

      ○ Do you want the article to be published and available for use on the site immediately after submission? If so, select the **Published** checkbox.

      ○ Do you want to promote the article to the front page? If so, select the **Promoted to front page** checkbox.

      ○ Do you want the article to remain at the top of the list of contents on the site? If so, select the **Sticky at top of list** checkbox.

   d. In the **Comments settings**, indicate whether you want to allow comments to be made on articles of this Content type or not, and if you do, then how these comments will be handled.

Do the same for all of the other new Content types. Now add some content to each category to ensure that you have done everything correctly.

**Tips and traps**

When a new Content type is created, you need to access the page for this Content type and deselect the **Promoted to front page** checkbox in the **Workflow settings,** or else any new content created gets promoted to the front page. This could cause you a lot of embarrassment when this occurs with inappropriate content.

If you think that your submission form needs more fields than the basic **Title** and **Body**, then you must install the **CCK** module, which will allow you to create them.

# Create new categories

Categories are used to classify items that fall under the same Content type and need to be grouped with others with which they bear closer similarity. For example, **News** is a Content type, but it can be further categorized into **Local**, **World**, and **Business** news. We must now create new categories and establish relationships between them and the new Content types. We will again create the **News** Content type and the content categories under it, as an illustration.

Navigate to the **Taxonomy** link under the **Content management** section of the **Administer** page, and click on it to get to the **Taxonomy** page. If you have started a new site, then you will see a notice that there is no vocabulary available for your new categories at the foot of this page. The **vocabulary** is a term by which a collection of categories (or terms) can be collectively described. In this case, let us create a vocabulary, which we will call **News**. We will do this by clicking on the link **Add vocabulary** at the top of the page. This is what we will be filling into the form for this new vocabulary.

1.  In the **Identification** fields, enter the of the **Vocabulary name**, a **Description**, as well as any **Help text** that comes to mind to guide the users when they come across this vocabulary. For **News**, we have used **News Type** as the vocabulary name, for the **Description** we have entered **The type of news that you are posting,** and for the **Help text** we will be instructing the user to **Select from list**.

2.  We need to associate this vocabulary with a Content type. We have created it specifically for News, so we naturally select the **News** checkbox.

3. For the **Settings**, we specify that the selection of a term from this vocabulary is **Required** and that the person posting the content must choose a term from the supplied list. Moreover, as we can have **Local**, **World**, and **Business** news, we select the **Multiple select** checkbox to indicate that multiple selections can be made. In other words, a posted content may have more than one term.

---

▽  Identification

**Vocabulary name:** *

News Type

The name for this vocabulary, e.g., *"Tags"*.

**Description:**

The type of news that you are posting

Description of the vocabulary; can be used by modules.

**Help text:**

Select from list

Instructions to present to the user when selecting terms, e.g., *"Enter a comma separated list of words"*.

▽  Content types

**Content types:**

☑ News

☐ Page

☐ Story

Select content types to categorize using this vocabulary.

▽  Settings

☐ Tags

Terms are created by users when submitting posts by typing a comma separated list.

☑ Multiple select

Allows posts to have more than one term from this vocabulary (always true for tags).

☑ Required

At least one term in this vocabulary must be selected when submitting a post.

**Weight:**

0  ▼

Vocabularies are displayed in ascending order by weight.

[ Save ]  [ Delete ]

---

On navigating back to the **Taxonomy** page, we see that the new vocabulary that we have just created is listed. Now we need to add the terms for the vocabulary.

| Name | Type | Operations | | |
|------|------|------------|------|------|
| News Type | News | edit vocabulary | list terms | add terms |

We do this by clicking on the **add terms** link and completing the form that you will be presented with. Forget the **Advanced options** link at the bottom at this stage, because we only have a single level of terms.

Do this for all of the other Content types. If you click on the **list terms** link on the vocabulary, then you will be presented with a list of the terms that you have created in the order that they will be presented to the user. If you don't like this order, then just drag the ones you want to change to the location that you want.

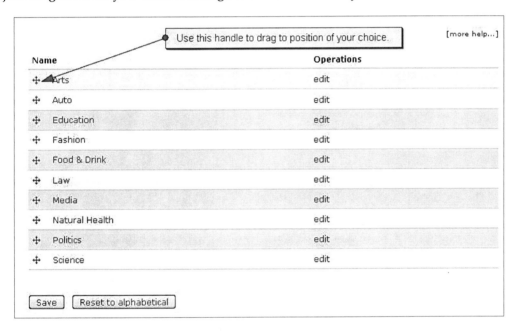

# Test the submission form

Now let us test our content submission form, and see how it works. In order to do this, click on the **Create content** link on the left, and select **News**. You will get a form similar to the one shown in the following screenshot:

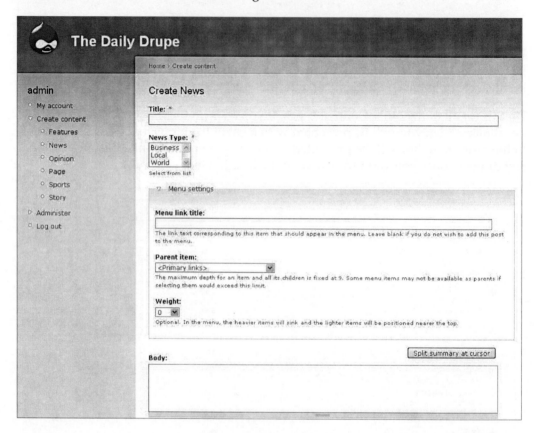

This form will enable you to submit your news. However, unless you know how to use HTML, there is no way to include images into your content. Therefore, we will enable the modules that make this possible.

# Images

We should now invoke some contributed modules from our list. Download the **IMCE** and **Image** modules, and install and enable them. While at it, also download the **TinyMCE** editor or any other editor of your choice, enable it, and configure it to your requirements. The TinyMCE editor is not essential. If you like a hard life, then you may want to continue to enter some of your content by using HTML. Finally, you must also enable the **Upload** module.

Having done this, now return to the **Administer | Content management | Content types** page, and select one of your new Content types. At the bottom of the page, you will see a new panel for **Image Attach settings**. Enable **Attach images**, and now your Content type will be ready to incorporate images. In order to confirm this, go to the **Create content** link again for the Content type and you will find the **Attached images** panel near the bottom end of the page, where you can upload images for your content.

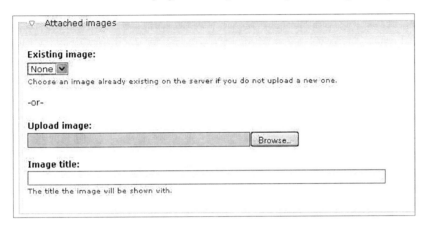

If you have also configured your TinyMCE editor correctly, then you should have an editor bar, similar to the one shown in the following screenshot, in the **Body** text area. You can also post images into the body of your article by using the image upload function in TinyMCE. However, if you use a different editor, then the display will be different but quite often as intuitive.

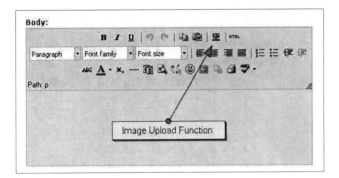

# Display content

Now that about settles much of what is required to post content into your web site. Let's look at how we may view what we have put in.

# Create quick menus with the Taxonomy Menu module

Again, there are several ways to display content. A quick and favorite method is to use a module known as **Taxonomy Menu**. This module is actually very useful. What it essentially does is it permits you to view the content on your site just by clicking on a menu link that corresponds to the title of a vocabulary term. Download the **Taxonomy Menu** module, and install it. Once it has been installed, browse to the **Administer** page and then on to the **Taxonomy Menu settings** page. Select the vocabularies that you want to include in your menu, and save the configuration. An overview of the settings on the **Taxonomy Menu settings** page can be seen in the following screenshot:

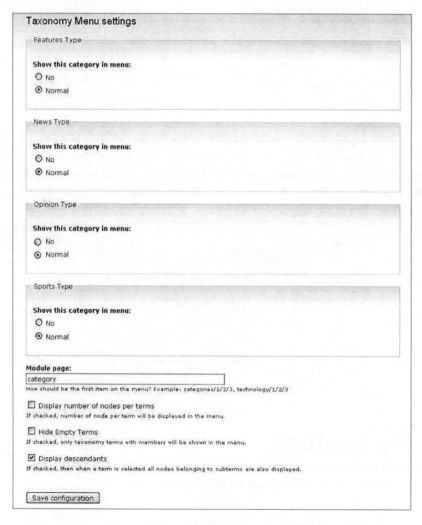

You will now see the links to the items related to each vocabulary term under the Navigation menu in the sidebar. If you have posted items into the categories already, then you will see that your posts appear on the page when you click on the corresponding menu. Navigate to the **Menus** page. Click on the **Navigation** link at the top of the page. On the resulting page, click on the **edit** link of each vocabulary listed and rename the **Menu link title** to **Features**, **News**, **Opinion**, and **Sports** respectively. Save the configuration and return to the Navigation menu. If you click on the **News | Local** link (shown in the following screenshot) for example, then it will show you a page containing all of the local news that has been posted to the site.

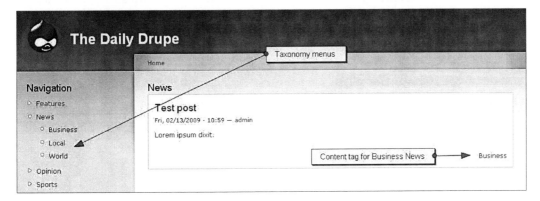

# Forums

Creating the forums should also be easy. Go to the **Modules** page, and enable the **Forum** module. On the **Forums** page in **Administer | Content Management,** you will be presented with a blank page. Here we will create a single Container that has only one single Forum. Let's call the container **General**, and the forum **Have your say**.

In order to do this, look for the links at the top of the page, and follow the instructions for creating the container and for creating the forum. The forum **Have your say** will have the container **General** as **Parent**.

| Name | Operations |
| --- | --- |
| ✛ General | edit container |
| ✛ Have your say | edit forum |

Save

Posting to the forum requires that you follow the process you must have become quite familiar with by now. Go to **Create content** link, and look for the **Forum topic** Content type. You will be presented with the form that you will recognize from the previous examples. Once you have completed this form, you will have created a forum topic. While at it, add a few more topics. You will find them useful in a few minutes.

# The lead story block

Next we will need to implement the requirement to view the "lead story", as well as the latest editorial, latest features, and latest local news, in blocks placed on the front page. Therefore, it is time to get acquainted with the **Views** module. Essentially, what this module does is provide a flexible method of controlling how lists of content are presented. After installing and enabling the module, visit the **Views** module on the **Administer** page.

When you first open the **Views** page, you may want to immediately take a quick dash out again, because it may look so unfriendly. But never mind, we will soon fall in love with it. With this module, we shall be creating:

- Latest editorial – block
- Lead story – block
- Latest features, listed as teasers – block
- Latest local news, as teasers – block

Let us start by creating the lead story block:

1. Click on the **Add** link at the top to add a new view
2. In this instance, add **leadstory** as **View name**, and select **View type** as **node**
3. The next screen is where the real battle will be fought:
   a. Select **Block** in the default setting
   b. In the **Basic settings**, give the block a **Title**, such as **lead story**
   c. In **Items to display**, change the value to **1**
   d. In **Fields**, select **Node: Title** and **Node: Teaser**
   e. In **Sort criteria**, select **Node: Published**, and choose descending order
   f. In **Filters**, select **Node:Type is one of Story**

The completed View page is shown in the following screenshot:

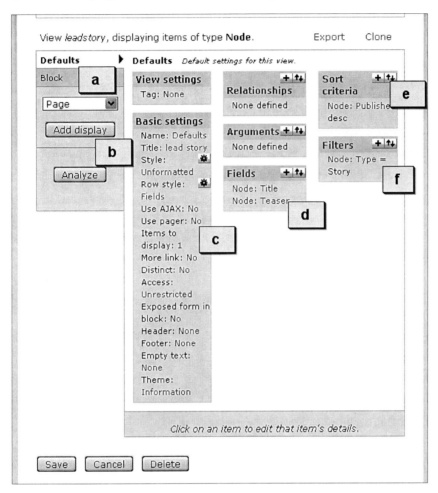

Save this, and you are done. If you now go to the **Blocks** page, then you will see that a new block has been created called **leadstory: Block**. When put in use, this block will display the title and teaser for the last article posted into the **Story** Content type, in a block. Now we are making good progress, right?

# The latest editorial block

In order to create this block, just follow the same procedure that we have just seen, but with a few changes:

a. Select **Block** in the default setting

b. In **Basic settings**, give the block a **Title**, such as **latest editorial**

c. In **Items to display**, change the value to **3**

d. In **Fields**, select **Node: Title** and **Node: Teaser**

e. In **Sort criteria**, select **Node: Published**, and choose descending order

f. In **Filters**, select **Node: Type is one of Editorial**

Save this, and you are done. If you now go to the **Blocks** page, then you will see that a new block has been created, called **latesteditorial: Block**. When put in use, this block will display the titles and teasers of the last three articles posted for the **Editorial** Content type, in a block.

# The latest features block

In order to create this block, just follow the same procedure that we have just seen, but with a few changes:

a. Select **Block** in the default setting

b. In **Basic settings**, give the block a **Title** such as **latest features**

c. In **Items to display**, change the value to **3**

d. In **Fields**, select **Node: Title** and **Node: Teaser**

e. In **Sort criteria**, select **Node: Published**, and choose descending order

f. In **Filters**, select **Node: Type is one of Features**

Save this, and you are done. If you now go to the **Blocks** page, then you will see that a new block has been created called **latestfeatures: Block**. When put in use, it will display the titles and teasers of the last three articles posted for the **Features** Content type, in a block.

# The latest news block

In order to create this block, just follow the same procedure we have been following, but with a few changes:

a.  Select **Block** in the default setting

b.  In **Basic settings**, give the block a **Title** such as **latest news**

c.  In **Items to display**, change the value to **3**

d.  In **Fields**, select **Node: Title** and **Node: Teaser**

e.  In **Sort criteria**, select **Node: Published**, and choose descending order

f.  In **Filters**, select **Node: Type is one of News**

Save this, and you are done. If you now go to the Blocks page, then you will see that a new block has been created called **latestnews: Block**. When put in use, this block will display the titles and teasers of the last three articles posted for the **News** Content type, in a block.

**Tips and traps**

In this example, all of the block displays are node titles and teasers. So if you don't want a display that will look like a mess, then you must tame the length of our teasers. For that, go to the **Administer** page and into the **Post settings** page, and set the length of trimmed posts. Better still, do this when you create your view, in the **Views** section.

You can also link the teaser **Title** field to its node and remove the **Label** text, in order to refine the look on the front page.

# Front page

There are several ways to create panels on the front page in the way required by the specifications. However, as we want to go to the pub in the next one hour, we will do it the easy way—by using the **Panels** module, which was surprisingly created to do exactly this kind of task.

1.  Install the **Panels 2** module, and enable it on the **Modules** page. You will find that a whole new section for **Panels** has been created on the **Administer** page, and this is where you set up your displays.

2. Click on **Panel pages**, and you will be presented with a blank page that shows that no panel has been created yet. Click on the **Add** tab at the top of the page to add a panel. This takes you to the configuration page, as shown in the following screenshot:

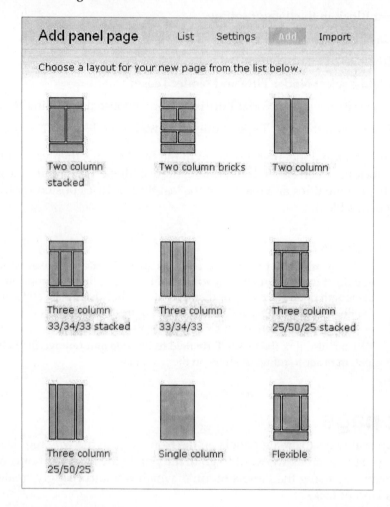

3. On this page, we can see that the arrangement that most closely resembles what we want is the **Two column stacked** display. Click on this option. On the page setting that comes up, add **front** in both the **Panel name** and **Path** fields and save. Ignore all of the other settings, and go to the **Content** settings. This is where you assign the blocks to the panel.

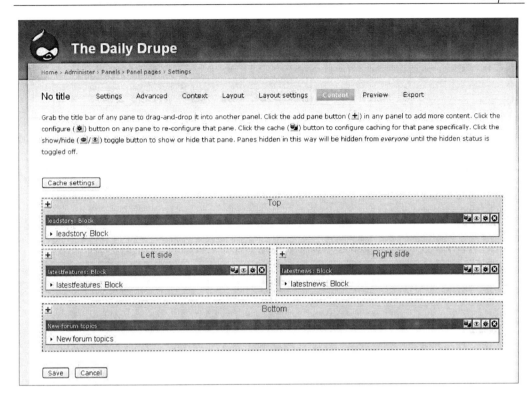

Assign the **leadstory, latestnews, latestfeatures**, and **new forum topics** to the panel, and set the default **Pane style** to **Rounded Corners**. Then click on **Save**.

The last thing to do before heading for the pub is to go to the **Site information** link on the **Administer** page, and change the default front page to **front**, which is the path of our panel, and save.

# Editorial and User login blocks

To place the **editorial** and **User login** blocks in the **Right sidebar**, we will visit the **Blocks** link on the **Administer** page. There, we will place both of the blocks in the **Right sidebar** (where we want them) and save the setting.

# Finishing up

We can now enable our new theme, **Analytic**, on the **Themes** page, and configure it to our preferences. Now, when we go to the front page, we see that our panel has replaced the content section on the front page, and we see that we are done with this project.

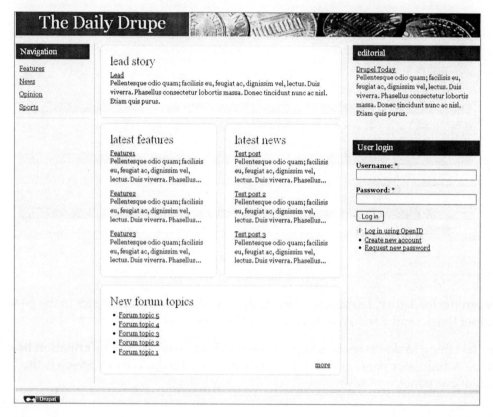

# Summary

In this chapter, you have learned how to:

- Build a basic site for publishing an online newspaper or magazine
- Use **Panels** and **View** modules effectively

In real life, you may want to increase the number of blocks to be displayed on the front page and sidebars. You may also want to create blocks for each Taxonomy term. As you can see, this is not so difficult when you are using the **View** module. You may also be envisaging a more elaborate layout on the front page and elsewhere on the web site. This is often easily done using the **Panels** module.

# 7

# Dridgets Inc.—Building an E-commerce Site

Dridgets Inc. are the foremost manufacturers of bespoke widgets in Drupelburg. Their 'dridgets' have won awards internationally and are considered vastly superior to other, mass-produced, widgets manufactured by so many unscrupulous garage factories. In order to consolidate their success, Dridgets have decided to set up an online e-commerce store to sell their dridgets. As a start, however, the widgets will only ship in Drupelburg and will be available in three colors—pink, yellow, and blue—and in only one size.

The functionality required by Dridgets for their web site includes:

- Simple page views of products from the links in the main menu
- A billing system with the automatic addition of a flat shipping cost for all items
- A shopping cart with checkout that permits payment by check or PayPal

Having considered other alternatives, Dridgets Inc. have chosen to use the Ubercart shopping cart for their web shop.

# Theme

The theme chosen is "Superclean", which is a Drupal community contribution. The front page will feature a two-column theme with the main content accommodating product information and the sidebar holding the blocks.

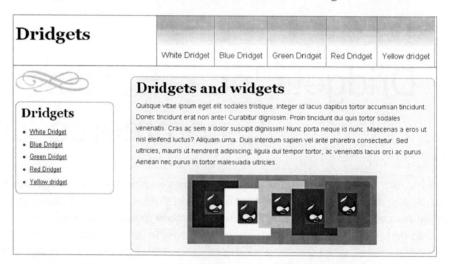

# Build the Dridgets Inc. web shop

Many books have been written on how to use Ubercart, and it will be foolhardy to imagine that everything about this very versatile shopping cart system can be learnt in a few pages. Therefore, we will look exclusively at the steps required to build the Dridgets Inc. project. Specifically we will be looking at how to:

1. Enable the shopping cart to list detailed product descriptions and images.

2. Show product name, detailed description, prices, and ordering procedure in full page view and with links to the main menu.

3. Configure product prices and billing to reflect the cost of flat-rate local shipping.

4. Configure the checkout to accept payment through PayPal.

# Modules

From the tasks that are presented by this project, we are able to build a list of contributed modules that will be used. The Dridgets web site will be built entirely around the Ubercart module. So for the purpose of this project, we shall be using the following modules:

# Optional Core modules

We will be using the following **Core** modules:

- **Taxonomy** — enables us to classify our content
- **Upload** — allows the upload of files and images into content

# Contributed modules

We will also be using the following contributed modules:

- **Ubercart** — the shopping cart on which the site will be based
- **Token** — provides an API for modules to use tokens
- **CCK** — allows custom fields to be added to nodes
- **Image** — allows users with the correct permissions to upload images
- **Image Field** — provides image upload field for CCK
- **Imagecache** — allows presets for image processing
- **Thickbox** — allows inline pop-ups for images

# Basic Ubercart configurations

Now, at first glance, Ubercart can look like a very hostile animal indeed, with many pages of daunting features. However, this needn't be so. Just imagine it as a feast, and you only need to take what you need from the whole table and leave the rest for later, or for other people with more varied tastes.

Firstly, we must enable Ubercart and all of the dependent modules, as indicated by the **Modules** table. Without the following modules Ubercart will not function, and so they must be enabled prior to installing Ubercart itself:

- **Token**

The following Ubercart modules from the **Core** grouping must be enabled for this particular project:

- **Cart** — provides the shopping cart for the Ubercart site
- **Order** — permits orders to be received and managed
- **Product** — allows products to be listed in the store
- **Store** — allows store settings to be implemented and for the site to be managed
- **Shipping Quotes** — displays shipping quotes information to customers at checkout

The following **extra** modules are also required to be enabled:

- **Flatrate**—charges a flat rate per product or per order for shipping
- **PayPal**—integrates PayPal services with Ubercart

For Ubercart to be able to configure core image support, enable the following modules:

- **Content**
- **CCK Image field**
- **Imagecache**

# Image configurations

This is not essential if you do not want images in your shopping cart catalog. However, without images, the web site will look very dreary indeed. Therefore, we will be adding image support. In order to do this, navigate to the main **Store administration** page at the URL `admin/store,` as shown in the following screenshot:

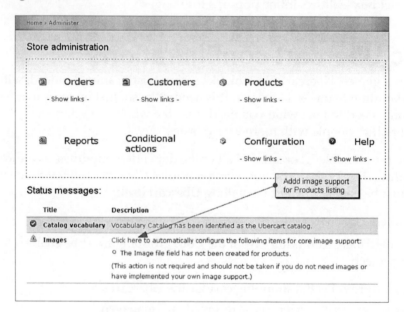

# Basic Store settings

To set the Basic Store settings, we go to the **Administer** page and, under **Store administration**, select the **Configuration** link that leads to the **Configuration** page. On this page, you will be presented with a selection of links. The ones that are most important at this stage are:

1. **Country settings** — where you define the countries that your store sells to.
2. **Payment settings** — where you determine how you want your customers to be able to pay.
3. **Store settings** — where you set some parameters such as your store's name, address, and associated information.

It is not that the other settings are less important, but as we observed earlier, Ubercart is a feast, and you should take what you need at any time rather than pile your plate with too much at once. Whenever you need to alter any of the other default settings, you may always return to do this.

# Country settings

Selecting the **Country settings** link will lead to the expected **Country settings** page. Select the **Import countries** link to give Ubercart the details of the countries that your cart will deal with. In this case, and only for the purpose of illustration, we have selected **United Kingdom**; **Canada** and the **United States** have been imported by default.

At this time, we will leave the **Country formats** setting at the default state.

# Payment settings

Selecting the **Payment settings** link will lead to the **Payment settings** page where you can configure your payment options. Here we are more interested in the **Payment methods** pane, and not because the others are not important. Just enough for the present serving, remember? Dridgets is using only **PayPal**, so we have selected PayPal.

In the **PayPal Websites Payment Standard settings** pane, as shown in the following screenshot, you can enter the details of your PayPal account so that, on checkout, the store will direct your customer to PayPal for a payment:

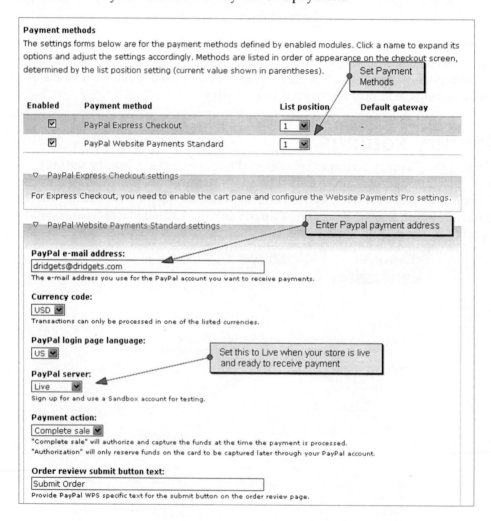

# Store settings

We do need to enlighten Ubercart, as well as the site users, on some stuff such as the store's name, address, and other information. Again, on the **Store settings** page, we will only be adding items that are listed on the **Contact settings** page, for simplicity.

**Store name:**

Dridgets Inc

**Store owner:**

Timi Ogunjobi

**E-mail address:**

mail@dridgets.com

☑ Include the store name in the from line of store e-mails.
May not be available on all server configurations. Turn off if this causes problems.

**Phone number:**

12323456789

**Fax number:**

**Street address 1:**

1 Dridgets Drive

**Street address 2:**

**City:**

Drupelburg

# Shipping quote settings

Now for another important aspect that we have nearly forgotten: after Joe Bling has ordered a dozen Dridgets and has been taken to the checkout point, he needs to be charged for shipping. Otherwise, Dridgets Inc. will lose out when getting the stuff to Joe Bling's house. Therefore, let's go to the **Shipping quotes settings** page to sort this out. Here, as we had earlier determined that all of the customers will be charged a flat rate of $2 per order for all of their purchases, we will select the **Flat Rate** tab on the **Quote methods** page.

We will be prompted to **Add a new flat rate shipping method,** and on clicking this link we will be led to a page similar to the following screenshot:

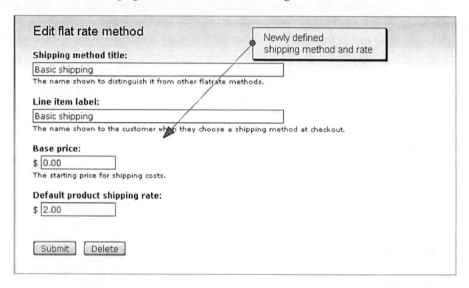

We have now created a new flat rate shipping method, which will charge every customer a basic rate of $2 for every single transaction, no matter the amount of the order.

# Image handling

In order to set up images for the Product Content type, we use the **Thickbox** module. Enable the module, and browse to the **Administer | Site configuration | Thickbox** page, to select the **Enable for image nodes** checkbox. Configure the **Product** Content type's **Ubercart product settings** panel to incorporate images for the **Product image field**.

# Add a Product to the store

When Ubercart is installed, it automatically creates a **Product** Content type. You may verify this by visiting the **Content types** link in **Administer**. If you are familiar with creating content (nodes) in Drupal, then you will know that to add a new node of type **Product**, you need to browse to the **Add content** link and select **Product**. This will give you the form required to submit your product descriptions.

## Create Product

**Name:** *

Name of the product.

| Split summary at cursor |

**Description:**

Enter the product description used for product teasers and pages.

▷ Input format

**Catalog:**

| - None - |

Hold Ctrl while clicking to select multiple categories.

▽ Product information

**SKU:** *

Product SKU/model.

**List price:**     **Cost:**     **Sell price:** *

$ [0]     $ [0]     $ [0]

The listed MSRP.     Your store's cost.     Customer purchase price.

☑ Product and its derivatives are shippable.

**Weight:**     **Unit of measurement:**

[0]     [Pounds ▼]

Dimensions

Physical dimensions of the packaged product.

**Units of measurement:** **Length:**     **Width:**     **Height:**

[Inches ▼]

**Package quantity:**

[1]

For a package containing only this product, how many are in it?

**Default quantity to add to cart:**

[1]

Leave blank or zero to disable the quantity field next to the add to cart button, if it is enabled in general. If it is disabled, this field is ignored.

**List position:**

[0 ▼]

Specify a value to set this product's position in product lists.
Products in the same position will be sorted alphabetically.

**Image:**

| Browse... | Upload |

✛     Maximum Filesize: *2 MB*
Allowed Extensions: *gif jpg jpeg png*

| Add another item |

In this **Product** form, we do not have to fill in all of the fields. Only the essential parts, such as the **Name**, **SKU**, and the product price, need to be completed. We should also enter an appropriate **Description** of the item and one or several photographs, or else we will find it a bit tough to get a potential buyer to purchase our invisible product. Note that these fields are essential because Ubercart demands that they be filled in. **SKU** stands for **Stock Keeping Unit**. It is the unique identifying mark for a specific product and thus must be defined. Without a price, nobody will be able to purchase the product. It may be helpful to add the product dimensions and the weight, so that the buyers have an idea of the size, especially if they are expecting it to fit in their mailbox.

Now post some products to make sure that your store has been properly set up. You should end up with a product page view similar to the one shown in the following screenshot:

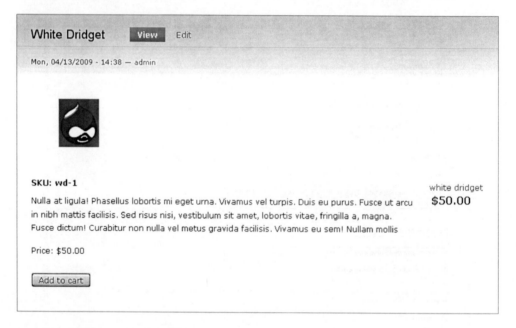

# Have we done this right?

We have configured the cart to accept payment, and we have added products to the cart. Let's see whether we have done this right by following a typical order process.

# Joe Bling selects a Dridget

The customer has clicked on the **Add to cart** button to buy a **Red Dridget**.

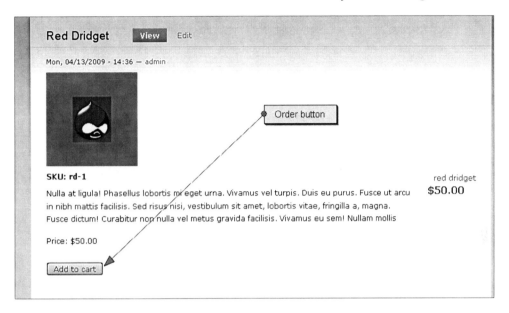

# Joe Bling is taken to the cart

Placing the order takes the customer to the cart, where he is given the options to **Continue shopping**, **Remove** the item from the cart, or proceed to the **Checkout**.

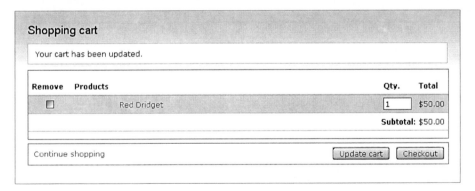

## Joe Bling goes for checkout

On deciding to go for checkout, the customer is taken to another page, where delivery and billing information is demanded.

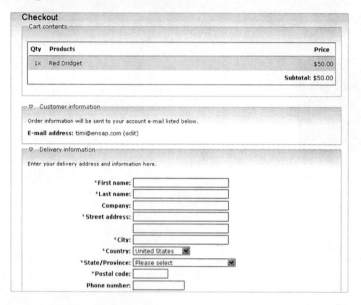

## Shipping cost calculated

The shipping cost will ordinarily be calculated from the delivery address, but as we have specified flat rate shipping, all customers will be charged the specified $2 per order.

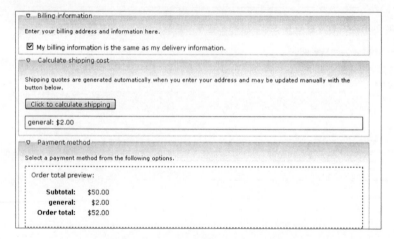

Clicking on the **Review Order** button at the bottom of this page takes the customer to the payment point. The order process has finally concluded.

# Display Products

This is a simple shopping cart with only one category of products, and there is no need for any elaborate menus and navigation systems. All we are looking to do is place links to each product page in the **Primary links** menu

In order to do this, we shall revisit each of the product pages, and click on the **Edit** tab. In the **Menu settings** section, we will enter the name of the product in the **Menu link title** field, and set the **Parent item** as **<Primary links>**.

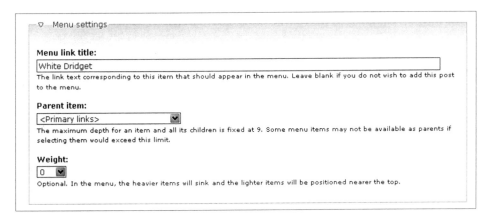

Now we need to put all of the links neatly together in a side bar. If we visit the **Blocks** page, then we will find a block for **Primary links**. Now we will move this block over to the **Left sidebar**, where we want it. We want to rename our menu **Dridgets**, so we go to the **configure** page for this block, and enter the new block title, before finally saving it. The result is that we have the new menu block displayed, as shown in the following screenshot:

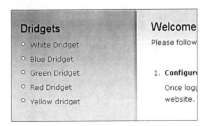

# Front page

The front page will be created from the **Page** Content type, as it only consist of some static text and image.

Click on the **Create content** link, and find the **Page** Content type. Start a new node titled **Dridgets and widgets**, and enter your text and images. When you are done, promote the node to the front page in **Publishing options**, and, in order to make sure that this post is not displaced by subsequent posts, also make it **Sticky at the top**, before saving. Otherwise, you could also browse to the **Site Information** link on the **Administer** page and make this node the default home page.

# Finishing up

We may now enable our new theme, **Superclean**, on the **Themes** page.

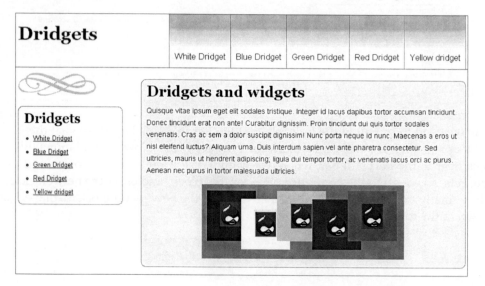

# Summary

In this chapter, you have learned how to:

1. Build a simple online shopping cart selling multiple products using Ubercart.

2. Configure the payment processing functionality using PayPal.

3. Define and implement the basic shipping method and cost parameters for the shopping cart.

# 8
# Drupelburg Accommodations—Building a Directory Site

Wally Fishbourne had the idea to create an online directory where people can freely post details of accommodation available for rent, share, and sale all over Drupelburg. He is looking for a simple directory, with listing and display features, rather than the style used in **Gumtree** and **Craigslist**. Users will be permitted to post without being registered.

The basic features of the Drupelburg Accommodations web site are:

- A front page view showing simple links to the following main sections:
    - Houses for rent (Offered and Wanted)
    - Houses to share (Offered and Wanted)
    - Houses for sale (In Drupelburg and Elsewhere)
- A simple listing form with taxonomy terms corresponding to the title sections.
- Sitewide search facilities.

# Theme

The theme chosen is "Zen Classic", which is a contributed theme with a simple and elegant look.

# Build Drupelburg Accommodations

Drupelburg Accommodations is another example of an easy-to-build web site, which can be completed within a couple of hours. The primary aim is to be able to access nodes that have been created, by means of their taxonomy, and also by means of sitewide search facilities. The major tasks involved in creating the Drupelburg Accommodations site will be:

- Creating new Content types for Accommodations
- Defining taxonomy terms relating to the listing categories and terms (Offered or Wanted)
- Creating menu blocks to view content based on listing categories and other taxonomy terms

# Modules

From the tasks that we are presented with by this project, we are able to build a list of contributed modules that will be used. For this exercise, we will be using the following modules:

# Optional Core modules

The **Core** modules that will be used for this site are as follows:

- **Taxonomy**—enables us to classify our content
- **Upload**—allows the upload of files and images into content

# Contributed modules

The contributed modules that will be used for this site are as follows:

- **Image**—allows users with the correct permissions to upload images. Thumbnails and additional sizes of images are created automatically.
- **IMCE**—gives the client ability to upload and manage some files through the Admin interface.
- **Panels**—needed to create multiple-column layouts in pages.
- **Taxonomy Menu**—permits the easy creation of menus from taxonomy vocabularies.
- **Poormanscron**—runs the Drupal cron operations without needing the cron application.

# Basic content

For the purpose of easy classification, we shall be creating three new Content types called **Accommodations for Rent**, **Accommodations to Share**, and **Accommodations for Sale**. This should make it easier for users to post their items onto the site, as well as make it a lot more straightforward to create a system for retrieving these items for display.

# Images

In order to permit images to be added to the content, get the **IMCE** and **Image** modules, and install and enable them. Finally, you must also enable the **Upload** module, otherwise users will not be able to attach images and other files to their posts.

# Create new Content type

By navigating to the **Administer** page of the site and then into the **Content management** section (shown in the following screenshot), we will find the **Content types** link.

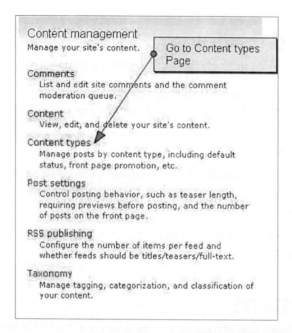

If we access this page, then we will see the various Content types listed. Here, we will create our own new Content type for **Accommodations for Rent**.

| Name | Type | Description | Operations |
|------|------|-------------|------------|
| | | We need to Create new content types | |
| Page | page | A *page*, similar in form to a *story*, is a simple method for creating and displaying information that rarely changes, such as an "About us" section of a website. By default, a *page* entry does not allow visitor comments and is not featured on the site's initial home page. | edit  delete |
| Story | story | A *story*, similar in form to a *page*, is ideal for creating and displaying content that informs or engages website visitors. Press releases, site announcements, and informal blog-like entries may all be created with a *story* entry. By default, a *story* entry is automatically featured on the site's initial home page, and provides the ability to post comments. | edit  delete |

In order to do this, we will use the following procedure:

1.  Click on the **Add content type** link at the top, and you will be presented with a form.

2.  Add the Content type descriptions and the general rules for the adding of content and the display of content for this new Content type in the places where they need to be in the form. Here are some guides:

    a. In the **Identification** fields, enter the **Name** and the **Description** of the Content type, as shown in the following screenshot:

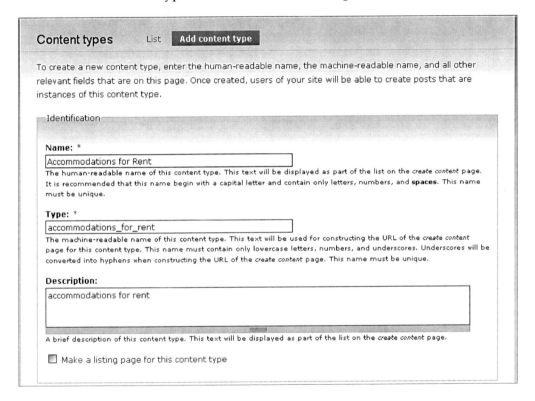

b. In the **Submission form settings** pane, choose the title that you want to give the fields. By default, you are presented with **Title** (for the title of the submission), **Body** (for the main story), as well as fields specifying the minimum length that an article must be before it can be accepted for submission. You will also find another place where you can describe submission guidelines for this Content type. Leave this at the system default setting.

c. In the **Workflow setting** pane, we need to determine the default options:

   ° Do you want the listing to be published and available on the site immediately after submission? If so, select the **Published** checkbox.

   ° Do you want to promote the listing to the front page? If so, select the **Promoted to front page** checkbox.

   ° Do you want the listing to remain at the top of the list of contents on the site? If so, select the **Sticky at top of list** checkbox.

d. In the **Comments settings** panel, you can indicate whether you want to allow comments to articles from this Content type or not, and if you do, then how these comments will be handled.

e. At the bottom of the page, you will see a new panel for **Image Attach settings** (shown in the upcoming screenshot). Enable **Attach images**, and now your **Accommodations for Rent** Content type will be ready to incorporate images. In order to confirm this, go to the **Create content** link for the Content type. Near the bottom of the page, you will find the **Attached images** panel, where you can upload images for your posts and decide how images will appear in the teasers and in the full node view, in terms of size and position.

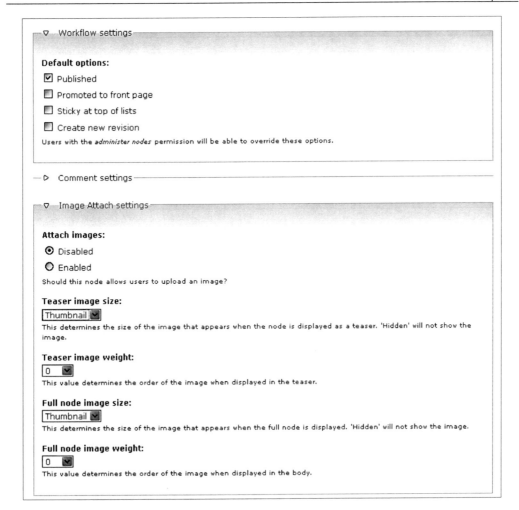

**Accommodations to Share** and **Accommodations for Sale** can be created using a similar procedure.

# Create new categories

Our accommodations will need to be organized into categories in order to group them together along with other houses, according to the listing type.

Go to the **Taxonomy** link under the **Content management** section on the **Administer** page, and navigate to the **Taxonomy** page. If you have started a new site, then you will see a notice that there is no vocabulary available for your new categories at the foot of this page. The **vocabulary** is a term by which a collection of categories (or terms) can be collectively described. In this case, let us create three vocabularies—**Houses for Rent, Houses to Share,** and **Houses for Sale**. we will do this by clicking on the **Add vocabulary** tab at the top of the page.

# List categories

This is what we will be filling into the form for this new vocabulary:

1. In the **Identification** panel, let us enter the **Name** of the vocabulary, a **Description**, as well as any **Help text** that comes to mind, to guide the users when they come across this vocabulary. For houses to rent, we have used **Houses for Rent** as the **Vocabulary name**; for the **Description**, we have entered **houses for rent**, and for the **Help text**, we will be instructing the user to **select from list**.

2. We need to associate this vocabulary with a Content type. We select the **Accommodations for Rent** checkbox.

3. For the settings, we declare that the selection of a term from this vocabulary is **Required**, and that the user who posts the content must choose a term from the supplied list.

We will follow the same procedure for the **Houses for Sale** and **Houses to Share** categories.

| | Name | Type | Operations | | |
|---|---|---|---|---|---|
| | | | | | [more help...] |
| ✛ | Houses for Rent | Accommodations for Rent | edit vocabulary | list terms | add terms |
| ✛ | Houses for Sale | Accomodations for Sale | edit vocabulary | list terms | add terms |
| ✛ | Houses to Share | Accommodations to Share | edit vocabulary | list terms | add terms |

Save

# Add terms

Going back to the **Taxonomy** page, we see that the new vocabulary that we have just created is listed. Now we need to add the terms for the **Houses for Rent** vocabulary, as well as for the other vocabularies. We do this by clicking on the add term link and completing the form that we are presented with, as shown in the following screenshot:

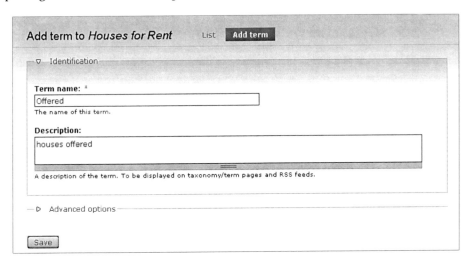

Ignore the **Advanced options** link at the bottom of the page at this stage, as we only have a single level of terms.

If you click on the **list terms** link on the vocabulary, then you will be presented with a list of the terms that you have created (seen in the upcoming screenshot), in the order that they will be presented to the user. If you don't like this order, then just drag the ones you want to change to the location that you want.

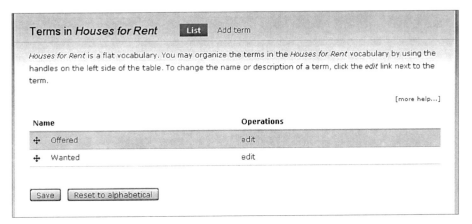

# Test the Houses for Rent submission form

Now let us test our submission form, and see how it works. In order to do this, we click on the **Create content** link on the lefthand side of the page, and select the **Houses for Rent** link. You will see a form that will have to be duly filled in, as shown in the following screenshot:

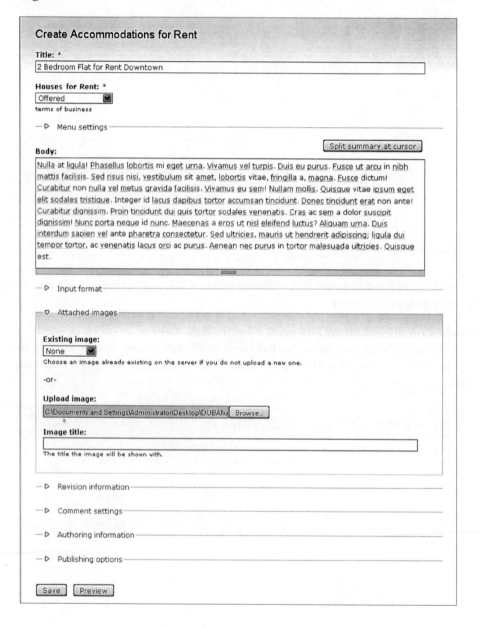

Now add some posts to all the Content types that you have created, to ensure that you have done it all correctly.

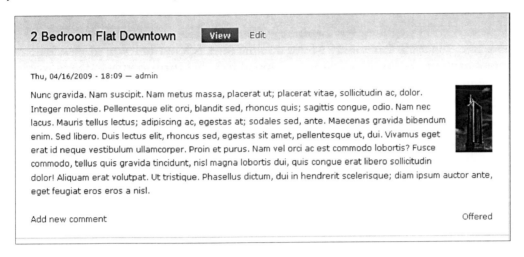

# Create postings

A single tab is available to create posts into the Drupelburg Accommodations site. The **Create posting** tab is obtained by renaming the **Create content** item in the **Navigation** menu and then moving this item to under the **Primary links** menu. In order to do this, access the **Menus** link on the **Administer** page, click on the **Navigation** link, and **edit** the **Create content** link to change the **Parent item** to **<Primary links>**. Save your new settings.

When the **Create posting** tab is clicked on, it will open a page listing all of the Content types that the user has been given permission to post into. The permissions are set, as usual, at the **Permission** page.

# Display content

The problem we now face is to be able to have a simple view of all of the houses listed on this site. Therefore, we will be creating a menu system that is more intuitive. We primarily need to create menu blocks for the front page. The blocks will be for:

- Houses for Rent (Offered and Wanted)
- Houses to Share (Offered and Wanted)
- Houses for Sale (In Drupelburg and Elsewhere)

# Create quick menus with the Taxonomy Menu module

Let us start off by enabling the **Taxonomy Menu** module and creating a simple menu tree. What the **Taxonomy Menu** module does is it permits you to view the content on your site just by clicking on a menu link that corresponds to the title of a vocabulary term. We will now set it to generate a menu for all of our taxonomy vocabularies and terms.

In order to do this, we navigate to the **Taxonomy Menu settings** link on the **Administer** page. This displays the page shown in the following screenshot:

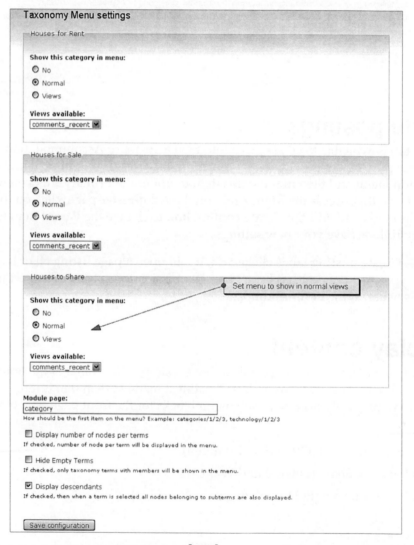

Select the vocabularies that you want to include in your menu, and save the configuration. In our example, we have selected all of them.

It is now time to go to the **Menus** page on the **Administer** page, where we will be doing a few special things. You will now see the **Taxonomy Menu** links to the items related to each vocabulary, in the **Navigation** link on this page, but we don't want it arranged this way.

What we are going to do is create three new menus for **Houses for Rent, Houses to Share**, and **Houses for Sale**. In order to do this, we will click on the **Add menu** tab at the top of the main **Menus** page.

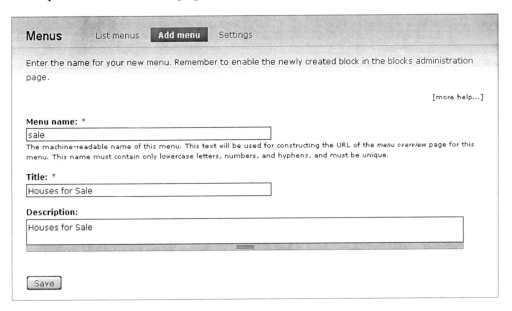

Now we will move all of the menu items that are currently under **Houses for Rent** in the **Navigation** menu, and place them under the new **Houses for Rent** menu. In order to do this, click on the **edit** link in front of **Houses for Rent**. In the resulting page, change the **Parent item** to **<Houses for Rent>**, and select the **Expanded** checkbox to expand the menu to make all child items visible.

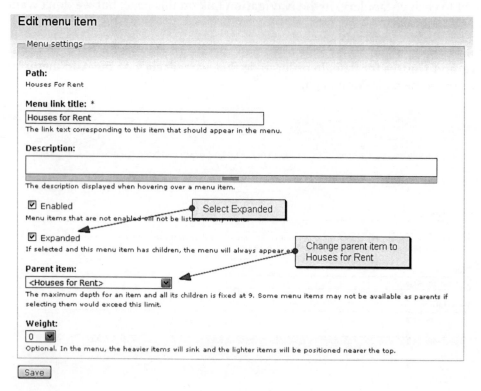

We shall do the same for the new **Houses to Share** and the **Houses for Sale** menus.

# Blocks

If we now visit the **Blocks** page on the **Administer** page, we should see that the blocks for **Houses for Rent**, **Houses for Sale**, and **Houses to Share** have been created. We want to move these to the front page—but not just yet.

# Front Panels

The front page will be created with the aid of the **Panels** module. This is one of the least—stressful methods of achieving the required layout. Install the **Panels** module, and enable it on the modules page. Now go to the **Panels** link on the **Administer** page, and access the main **Panels** configuration page.

Click on the **Panel pages** link, and you will be presented with a blank page that shows that no panel has been created yet. Click on the **Add** tab at the top of the page to add one. This leads to a page showing the various arrangements available to you, as shown in the following screenshot:

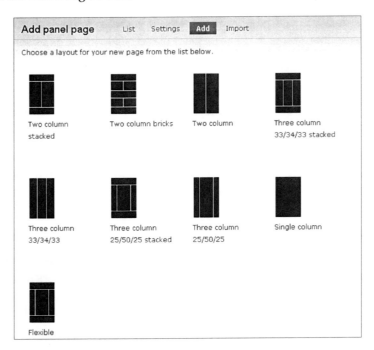

From this page, we see that the arrangement that most closely resembles what we want is the **Three column** display. Click on this layout option. On the page that is displayed next, add **front** in both the **Panel name** and **Path** fields, and then save your changes. Ignore all of the other settings, and go to the **Content** settings. This is where you assign the blocks to the panel.

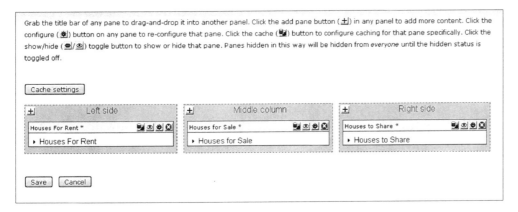

Assign the **Houses for Rent**, **Houses for Sale**, and **Houses to Share** blocks to their respective panels. We can also set the **Pane style** to **Rounded corners**. Then click on the **Save** button.

Now we shall quickly go to the **Site information** section on the **Administer** page, and change the default front page to **front**, which is the path field of our panel, and then save our changes.

# Search

Before setting up the search functionality, you need to enable the **Poormanscron** and **Search** modules.

After doing this, go to the **Administer | Site building | Blocks** page, and drag the **Search** block to the footer, where we want it. We can also navigate to the **Administer** page, and configure **Poormanscron** to carry out cron runs.

# Permissions

For the site to run the way that you want, user permissions will need to be set. You will need to set privileges such as posting and search. Because users are not required to register before making posts, it is a wise idea to moderate all of the posts by preventing automatic publishing of posts. This will assure that your site does not quickly become crippled by spam.

The **User login** block will not be used, so we will hide by assigning the **Region** to <none> on the **Administer | Site building | Blocks** page.

# Finishing up

We can now enable our new theme, **Zen Classic**, on the **Themes** page, to finish up our project.

# Summary

In this chapter, you have learned how to:

- Build a basic directory site
- Demonstrate how to Create multiple column page layouts using the **Panel** module

# 9

# Nosh'r—Building a Photo Sharing Site

William and Elizabeth Bunter are organizing an online food appreciation community. They intend to enroll members from all over the world to share their food photos on their new web site—Nosh'r. At Nosh'r, the users will submit photos of their food for all of the other members to admire and rate by means of stars. Photos will be classified into several categories: starters, main courses, desserts, and drinks.

The Nosh'r web site will have the following features:

- Photo galleries for several food categories (starters, main courses, desserts, drinks)
- A simple photo uploading form, which will also permit detailed descriptions of uploaded items
- A star rating system and comment form for each added contribution

# Theme

The theme chosen and for no particular reason other than it fits the project is "Magazeen", which is a contributed theme.

# Build Nosh'r

Billy and Bessie, as they are fondly known by their many friends from all over the world, will do anything for the promotion of gastronomic delights, and Nosh'r is a child of their zeal. On this web site, registered users will be permitted to blog pictures of the exciting foods and drinks that they have just consumed (taken before the food and drink are consumed), or that they have just discovered in an exotic eating place somewhere in the world. These photos will typically be accompanied by a description or a recipe and will be displayed in an image gallery on the web site with facilities for other members to judge the contribution by means of a five-star rating system.

Looking at this project more closely, we will see that it bears a lot of similarity to the blogging site, albeit with a different set of modules. For this web site to become a reality, we need to do the following:

- Create an image gallery
- Enable primary tagging of food images by continent of origin and class of food (starters, main courses, desserts, and drinks)
- Enable the free-tagging of images by country and other user-defined terms
- Enable the rating of and commenting on submitted food images

# Modules

From the defined tasks for this project, we should immediately see that there are some modules that are quite necessary. As usual, there are often several ways of getting the same result, each method undoubtedly with its own merits. However, for the purpose of this example, we shall be using the following modules:

## Optional Core modules

We will be using the following **Core** modules enabled via the **Modules** page:

- **Taxonomy** — enables us to classify our content
- **Comment** — permit users to comment on pictures

## Contributed modules

We will also be using the following contributed modules, which will be uploaded and then enabled via the **Modules** page:

- **Image** — allows users with the correct permissions to upload images. Thumbnails and additional sizes of images are created automatically.
- **Taxonomy Menu** — transform taxonomy vocabularies into menus easily.
- **Fivestar** — enable the rating of content using stars or similar icons.

# Configure the Fivestar module

The **Fivestar** module makes it easy for site users to vote on a node—in this case an image. It also includes a comments form for the optional addition of comments. We can access the **Fivestar settings** page from **Administer | Site Configuration | Fivestar**. The basic setting is to select the type of widgets that we want to use, from the **Widget display** menu, as shown in the following screenshot:

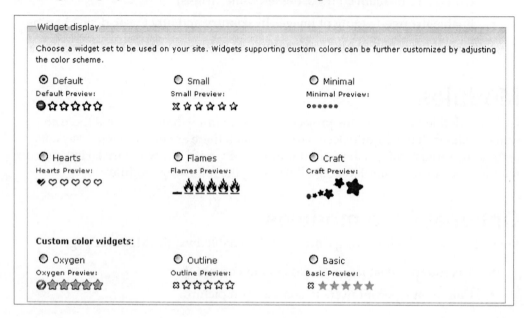

We have chosen to use the **Default** star widget for use on this site.

# Basic content

The site is built around the **Image** module, and the main challenge of this project will be to configure the image gallery to make the content quickly accessible.

# Create Images and galleries

Download, install, and enable the **Image** module. The **Image Gallery** functionality should also be enabled.

# Configure the Image Content type

The **Image** Content type is automatically created when the **Image** module is enabled. This Content type will permit users to post images into the site.

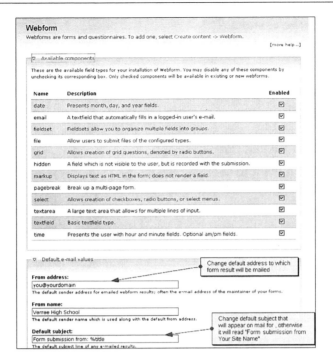

By navigating to the **Administer** page of the site and then into the **Content management** section, we will find the **Content types** link. If we access this page, then we will see the various Content types listed there. We will not be creating a new Content type, as the **Image** Content type (shown in the following screenshot) is already present.

To configure the **Image** Content type:

1.   Click on the **edit** link at the top of the **Image** Content type; you will then be presented with a form.

2.   In the **Workflow setting** pane, we need to determine the default options:

     °   Do you want the image to be published and made available for use on the site immediately after submission? If so, select the **Published** checkbox.

     °   Do you want to promote the image to the front page? If so, select the **Promoted to front page** checkbox.

     °   Do you want the image to remain at the top of the list of contents on the site? If so, select the **Sticky at top of list** checkbox. For this example, we will not select this option.

3.   In the **Fivestar ratings** pane, there are several configurable options from the primary need to enable Fivestar ratings, to other factors such as the number of stars to display, whether the widget will be placed below or above the node content, and also whether the rating of comments is permitted.

4.   In the **Comments settings** pane, indicate whether you want to allow comments to be made on images or not, and if you do, then how these comments will be handled.

# Create the Image galleries

Our images will need to be organized into galleries in order to group them together with other similar images according to the type of food.

Browse to the **Image galleries** link under the **Content management** section on the **Administer** page, and navigate to the **Image galleries** page. If you have started a new site, then you will see at the foot of this page a notice that there are no galleries available yet. We are going to create new galleries for starters, main courses, desserts, and drinks. We will do this by clicking on the **Add gallery** at the top of the page. This is what we will be entering into the form for this new gallery:

1.   In the **Identification** panel, enter the **Gallery name**, a **Description**, and also any **Help text**. For drinks, we have used **Drinks** as the gallery name. For the **Description**, we have entered **All drinks go down well here**.

2.   We need to establish a relationship between this gallery and the rest of the galleries. However, as it stands on its own, we define it as a **<root>** gallery.

When all of the galleries have been added, click on the **List** tab at the top of the page. We will arrive at a page listing all of the galleries available, as shown in the following screenshot:

# Image Taxonomies

We are now able to organize our images into separate galleries and group them together with other similar images according to the type of food. However, we additionally need to be able to group the images according to the continent of origin as well as other terms that may be defined by the site users.

Navigate to the **Taxonomy** link under the **Content management** section on the **Administer** page, and click on it to navigate to the **Taxonomy** page. Here we see that a vocabulary titled **Image Galleries** has been created, with terms such as **Drinks**, **Desserts**, **Main courses**, and **Starters**.

The **vocabulary** is the name by which a collection of categories (or terms) can collectively be described.

In this case, let us create two vocabularies—**Continent** and **Other Tags**. We will do this by clicking on the **Add Vocabulary** tab at the top of the page. The fields in the form for the **Continent** vocabulary will be filled in as follows:

1. In the **Identification** panel, enter the **Vocabulary name**, a **Description** and also any **Help text** that comes to mind, to guide the users when they come across this vocabulary. For continent, we have used **Continent** as the **Vocabulary name**. For the **Description**, we have entered **The continent that you are posting from**, and for the **Help text**, we will be instructing the user to **Enter the continent which you are posting from**.

2. We need to associate this vocabulary with a Content type. We have created it specifically for Images, so we naturally select the **Image** checkbox in the **Content types** pane.

3. For the **Settings**, we declare that the selection of a term from this vocabulary is **Required**, and the user who posts the content must choose a term from the supplied list.

Whereas the vocabulary **Continent** will have terms included for selection, the **Other Tags** vocabulary is free-tagging, which means the person making the submission will fill these in by himself or herself.

The following screenshot shows the values entered in the fields for the
**Continent** vocabulary:

| Taxonomy | List | **Add vocabulary** |

Define how your vocabulary will be presented to administrators and users, and which content types to categorize with it. Tags allows users to create terms when submitting posts by typing a comma separated list. Otherwise terms are chosen from a select list and can only be created by users with the "administer taxonomy" permission.

[more help...]

▽  Identification

**Vocabulary name:** *

Continent

The name for this vocabulary, e.g., *"Tags"*.

**Description:**

The continent that you are posting from

Description of the vocabulary; can be used by modules.

**Help text:**

Enter the continent which you are posting from

Instructions to present to the user when selecting terms, e.g., *"Enter a comma separated list of words"*.

▽  Content types

**Content types:**

☑ Image

☐ Page

☐ Story

Select content types to categorize using this vocabulary.

▽  Settings

☐ Tags
Terms are created by users when submitting posts by typing a comma separated list.

☐ Multiple select
Allows posts to have more than one term from this vocabulary (always true for tags).

☑ Required
At least one term in this vocabulary must be selected when submitting a post.

**Weight:**

0 ▾

Vocabularies are displayed in ascending order by weight.

Save

Going back to the **Taxonomy** page, we see the new vocabulary that we have just created listed. Now we need to add the terms for the **Continent** vocabulary. We do this by clicking on the **add terms** link and completing the form that we are presented with. Ignore the **Advanced options** link at the bottom of the page at this stage, because we only have a single level of terms.

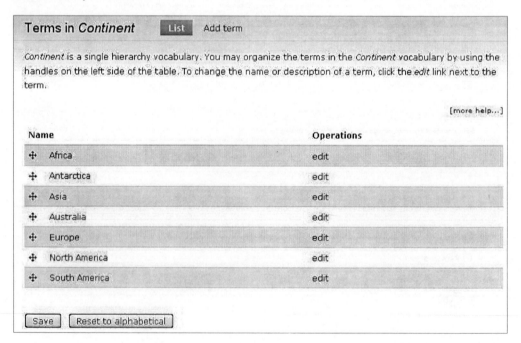

If you click on the **list terms** link of the vocabulary, you will be presented with a list of the terms that you have created (in the order that they will be presented to the user). If you don't like this order, then just drag the ones you want to change to the location that you want.

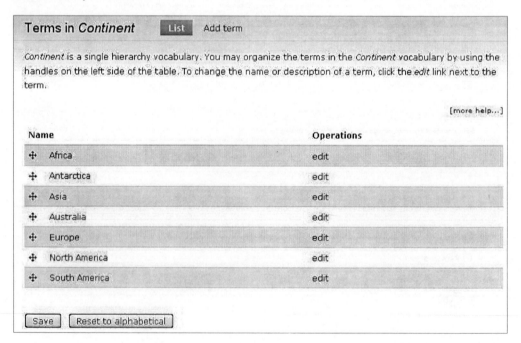

# Test the Image submission form

Now let us test our Image submission form, and see how it works. In order to do this, click on the **Create content** link in the Navigation menu and select **Image**. You will see a form, similar to the one shown in the following screenshot, which can be duly filled in:

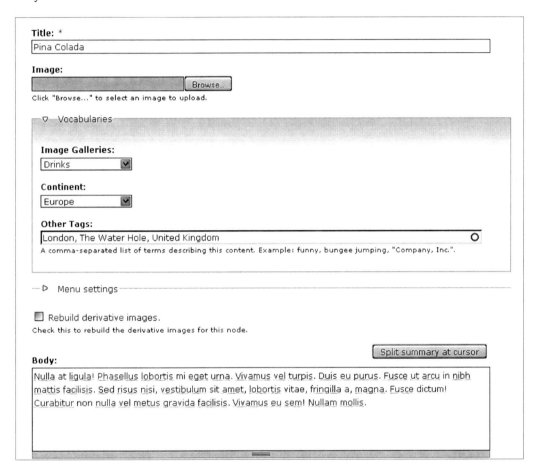

Now add some images to ensure that you have done everything correctly.

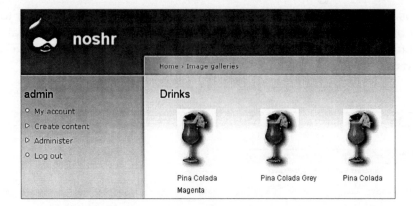

>
>
> **Tips and traps**
> Remember to change the permissions to create Image and upload files
> in the **Permissions** link on the **Administer** page.

# Display content

We have learnt how to post Images into the gallery. Now let us classify our Images
by the **Image Galleries** food type, and then by **Continent**.

# Create quick menus with the Taxonomy Menu module

As before, there are several ways to provide quick access to images via their
vocabulary. One quick method is to use a module known as **Taxonomy Menu**. What
this essentially does is permits you to view your Images simply by clicking on a
menu link that corresponds to the title of a vocabulary term.

Download the **Taxonomy Menu** module and install it. After this, go to the
**Administer** page and then onto the **Taxonomy Menu settings** page. Select the
vocabularies that you want to include in your menu, and save the configuration.
For our example, the **Taxonomy Menu settings** page should be configured as shown
in the following screenshot:

**Taxonomy Menu settings**

Continent

**Show this category in menu:**

○ No

◉ Normal

Image Galleries

**Show this category in menu:**

○ No

◉ Normal

Other Tags

**Show this category in menu:**

◉ No

○ Normal

**Module page:**

`category`

How should be the first item on the menu? Example: categories/1/2/3, technology/1/2/3

☐ Display number of nodes per terms

If checked, number of node per term will be displayed in the menu.

☐ Hide Empty Terms

If checked, only taxonomy terms with members will be shown in the menu.

☑ Display descendants

If checked, then when a term is selected all nodes belonging to subterms are also displayed.

[ Save configuration ]

You will now see the links to the items related to each vocabulary under the Navigation menu in the sidebar. If you have posted items into the categories already, then you will see that your posts appear on the page when you click on the corresponding menu. If you click on the **Continent | Africa** link, for example, then you will see a page containing Images that have been posted to the site from Africa.

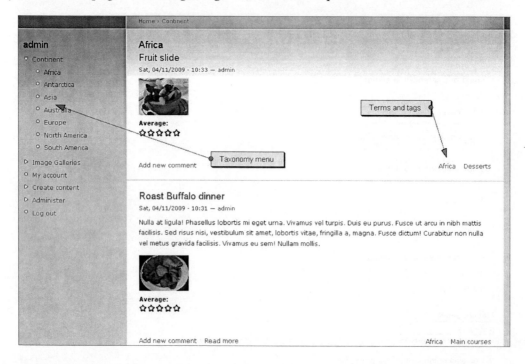

# Latest Image block

In the **Blocks** link on the **Administer** page, we will find that blocks have been automatically created for latest image submitted. We will now assign the **Latest image** block to the **Right sidebar**, as we had planned.

# Site navigation

Now let's tidy up our site by creating a menu system that is more intuitive. We will:

- Put our entire **Continent** menu under a newly-created **Grub** menu
- Assign the gallery to the front page

# Create the Menu for Continent and Galleries page views

In order to do this:

1. Navigate to the **Menus** link on the **Administer** page.

2. Click on the **Add menu** tab to access the page to create the menu.

3. Add a new menu called **Grub.**

4. Click on the **Navigation** link at the top of the **Menus** page to access the page that lists all of the navigation links.

5. Click on the **edit** link in front of the vocabulary **Continent**.

6. On the resulting page, change the **Parent item** to **<Grub>**, and also select the **Expanded** checkbox, as shown in the following screenshot:

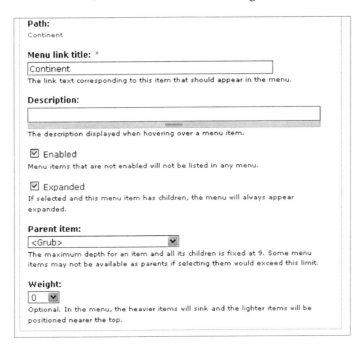

After saving, you are taken to another page, which shows that all of the menu items for the terms have been moved to under **Grub**. Do the same for the **Image Galleries** link.

Now visit the **Blocks** page, grab the **Grub** block, and drag it to the **Right sidebar** section of the regions list. On saving the settings, you will see that your new **Grub** links for **Continent** and for **Image Galleries** have been neatly placed where they can be accessed easily.

## Assign the Gallery to the front page

In order to assign the Gallery to the front page, go to the **Site information** link on the **Administer** page. At the foot of the page, we will find the field to set the **Default front page**. The view page for the **Image gallery** is image, so we can change the setting to **image**, as shown in the screenshot below:

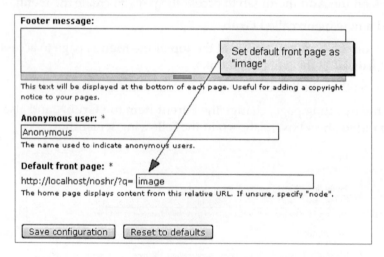

# Finishing up

We can now enable our **Magazeen** theme on the **Themes** page.

# Summary

In this chapter, you have learned how to:

- Build a basic site for publishing images uploaded by various users
- Use defined terms and free-tagging to classify content

# 10
# Drupelburg Conference Venues—Building a Conference Facilities Booking Site

**Drupelburg Conference Venues (DCV)** has been organizing conferences and events for many years. They have realized that much of their operation may be eased and much of their overheads reduced if they had a web presence. DCV is contemplating creating a web site where facilities can be listed and booked in real time. The site will be built in a way that makes it easy for the staff of DCV to list and update the venues.

The main features of the DCV web site will be as follows:

- Permitted users (the employees of DCV) will be able to list venues and add photographs
- A review system for the facilities to guide general site users

# Theme

The theme chosen is "Four Seasons", which is a contributed theme.

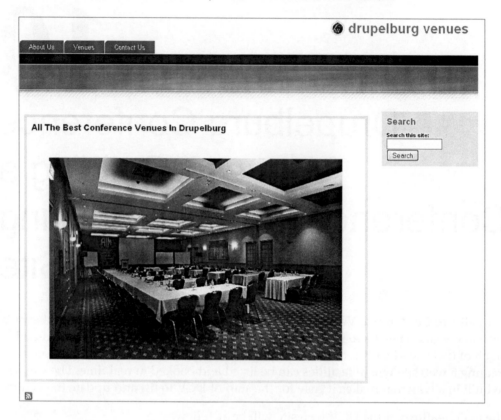

# Build Drupelburg Conference Venues

The DCV web site is (when we look very closely) a basic Drupal site with the nodes (articles) defining an object—a conference venue. The prominent additions are a means of defining the availability of the venue and also a means to comment on it and award star ratings.

Thus, the major tasks involved in the creation of this web site will be:

- Creating a new Content type titled "Venue"
- Adding availability features
- Adding the five-star rating system
- Adding a link to contact the facility owner
- Adding a comments form

# Modules

From the tasks that are presented to us by this project, we are able to build a list of contributed modules that will be used. There are often several ways of getting the same result, with each method undoubtedly requiring different combinations of contributed and core modules. However, for the purpose of this example, we shall be using the following modules:

## Optional Core modules

We will be using the following **Core** modules , which can be enabled via the **Modules** page:

- **Taxonomy** — enables us to classify our content
- **Comment** — permits users to comment on venues

## Contributed modules

We will also be using the following contributed modules from `Drupal.org`. Install, and enable them via the **Modules** page:

- **Image** — allows users with the correct permissions to upload images. Thumbnails and additional sizes of images are created automatically.
- **Availability** — allows availability information to be displayed for specified Content types by using calendars.
- **Fivestar** — a simple five-star voting widget for nodes.
- **SimpleViews** — an easy-to-use tool for building content listing pages.
- **Views** — allows the creation of customized lists and queries from the database.
- **Poormanscron** — automates the cron function.

# Configure the Availability Calendars module

The **Availability Calendars** module allows nodes to be turned into bookable items, and indicates the availability of the item at any particular time. Visit the **Availability Calendars** link on the **Administer** page to access the configuration page (shown in the following screenshot) for this module.

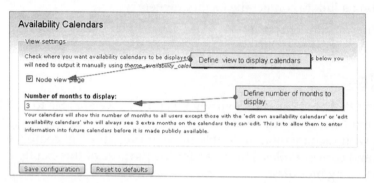

On this page, we want the calendars to show up in the **Node view page** and also want it to show for **3** months at a time.

# Configure the Fivestar module

The **Fivestar** module will make it easy for the site users to vote on a node — in this case a listed facility. It also includes a comments form for the optional addition of an opinion on the facility. The basic setting here is to select the type of widgets that we want to use from the **Widget display** page, shown in the following screenshot:

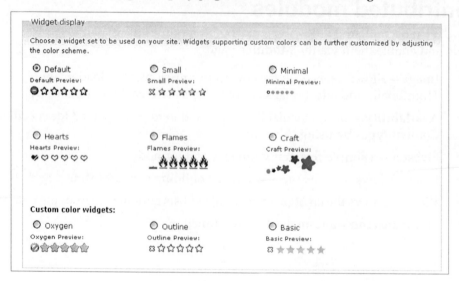

We have chosen to use the **Default** star widgets for this web site.

# Basic content

For ease of classification, we shall be creating a new **Venue** Content type. This will leave the core Content types free for any other use, such as a description of the activities of the company, or the features of the site.

# Create a new Content type

By navigating to the **Administer** page of the site and then into the **Content management** section, we will find the **Content types** link. Click on this link.

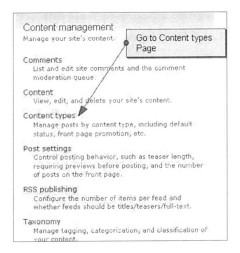

On the **Content types** page, we will see the various Content types that available for this site. We will need to create our own new Content type for **Venue**.

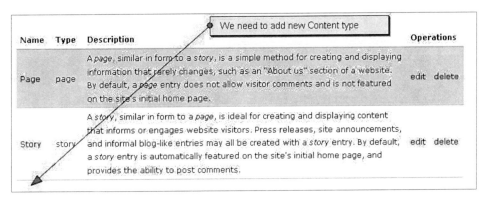

In order to create the **Venue** Content type:

1. Click on the **Add content type** link at the top of the page, and you will then be presented with a form.

2. Add the Content type descriptions and the general rules for adding content and the display of content for this new Content type (in the places where they need to be in the form). Here are some guides:

   a. In the **Identification** fields, add the **Name** and **Description** of the Content type.

   b. In the **Submission form settings**, you need to decide on the title that you want to give the fields. By default, you are presented with **Title** (for the title of the submission), **Body** (for the main story), as well as fields specifying the minimum length that an article must be before it can be accepted for submission. We are also provided with a place to describe the submission guidelines for this Content type. Leave this set to the system default setting.

   c. In the **Fivestar ratings** panel, there are several configurable options — from the primary need to enable Fivestar ratings, to other factors such as the number of stars to display, whether the widget will be placed below or above the node content, and also whether the rating of comments is permitted.

The following screenshot shows the **Fivestar ratings** pane with the settings configured:

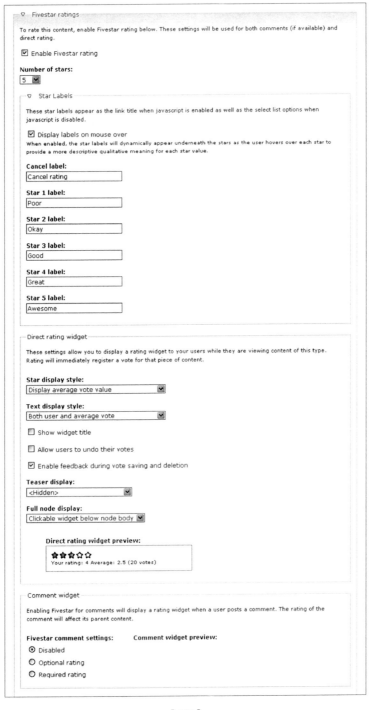

d. In the **Workflow setting** panel, we need to determine the following default options:

- ° Do you want the venue to be published and made available for use on the site immediately after submission? If so, select the **Published** checkbox.

- ° Do you want to promote the venue to the front page? If so, select the **Promoted to front page** checkbox.

- ° Do you want the venue to remain at the top of the list of contents on the site? If so, select the **Sticky at top of list** checkbox.

- ° Do you want the Content type to have Availability Calendar support? In that case, we select the **Enabled** checkbox.

- ° Do you want the nodes of this type to show the contact the author link at the bottom? If so, select the **Enabled** checkbox.

e. In the **Comments settings** tab, you can indicate whether you want to allow comments to be made on articles of this Content type or not, and if you do, then how these comments will be handled.

---

**Tips and traps**

When a new Content type is created, you need to access the page for this Content type and disable the **Promoted to front page** option in the **Workflow settings**, or else any new content created will be promoted to the front page, which could cause you a lot of embarrassment when this occurs with inappropriate content.

If you think that your submission form needs more fields than the basic **Title** and **Body**, then you must install the **CCK** module, which will allow you to create them.

---

# Images

If you attempt to add content to the newly-created **Venue** Content type, then you will find that the form has no place to incorporate images. In order to permit images to be added to the content, the **Image** module needs to be enabled.

Having done this, return to **Administer | Content management | Content types**, and check the **Venue** Content type page again. At the bottom of the page, you will see a new panel for **Image Attach settings**. Enable **Attach images**, and now your **Venue** Content type will be ready to incorporate images. In order to confirm this, go to the **Create content** link again for the **Venue** Content type, and you will find the **Attached images** panel, near the bottom end of the page, where you can upload images for your Venues.

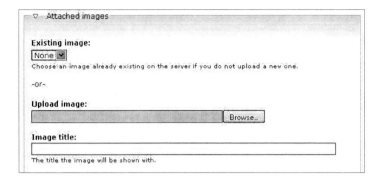

# Test the Venue submission form

Now let us test our Venue submission form and see how it works. In order to do this, click on the **Create content** link on the leftmost side of the screen, and select **Venue**. You will see a form similar to the one shown in the following screenshot:

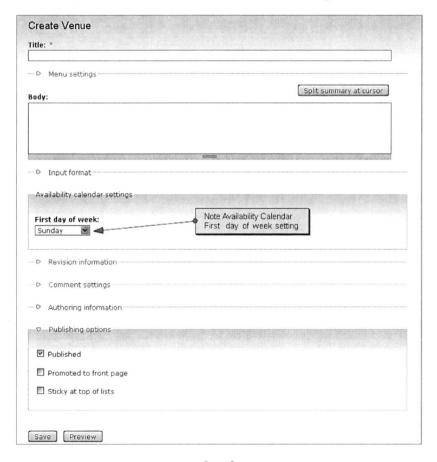

Now add some posts to ensure that the **Venue** Content type has been configured properly.

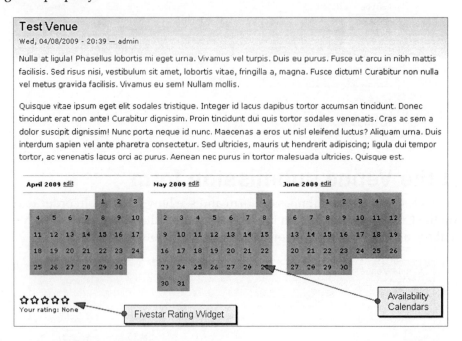

# Edit the Availability Calendar

If you look at the top of each month of the calendar, then you will see an **edit** link. This link will enable you to set the availability of the Venue for each day of the month. When you click on the link, you will arrive at following page, which lists all of the weeks and days of the month that we are addressing. The selectable options available are: **Fully booked** and **Provisionally booked**, and you must have one of these for every day. The result of the editing is shown in the following screenshot:

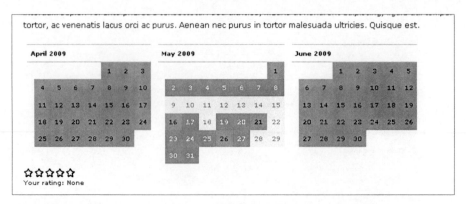

**Tips and traps**

Remember to change the permissions to **create venue content**, **create images**, and **upload files** in the **Permissions** link on the **Administer** page.

# Display content

We are looking to create a simple view of all of the venues listed on this site, and this is why we have chosen the **SimpleViews** module. In order to configure this module, we access the **SimpleViews** page from the **Administer** page, and from there select the relevant options, as seen in the following screenshot, to generate a simple list view for the **Venue** Content type:

# Quick searching

The **Search** module provides a form through which the entire site can be searched based on a keyword that the user provides. Enable this module. Go to the **Blocks** page, and put it in the region that suits you. In this case, we have placed it at the top of the **Right sidebar**.

Do make sure that the **Poormanscron** module has also been enabled, or else the search facility will not function as it should.

# Other pages

The other pages needed on this web site are:

- The **About us** page, which describes the activities of DCV
- The **Contact us** page, which lists all of the key contact addresses for DCV

Both of these pages can quickly be created from the **Page** Content type. We will add menu links to both pages and the **Primary link** menu as the nodes are created.

# Menus

We will now create a menu system that is more intuitive. For simplicity, we will also put our newly-created page view for **venues** under the **Primary link** menu.

In order to do this, go to the **Menus** link on the **Administer** page.

1. Click on **Primary links** to list all of the links in that menu.

2. On the resulting page, click on the **Add item** tab at the top.

3. Add the newly-created view page for **venues** to the **Primary links**, as shown in the following screenshot:

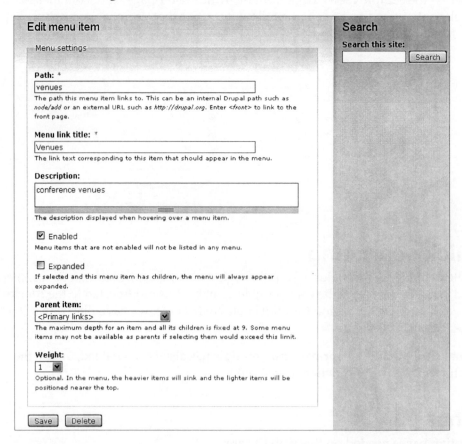

After saving, you are taken to an updated page for all of the menu items under the **Primary links** menu.

# Login and Navigation blocks

Because the only users who are permitted to enter content into this web site are the employees of DCV, the Login and Navigation blocks have been hidden. This is done by visiting the **Blocks** link on the **Administer** page and setting the **Region** to **<none>**.

# Finishing up

We can now enable our new theme, **Four Seasons**, on the **Themes** page to finish up our project.

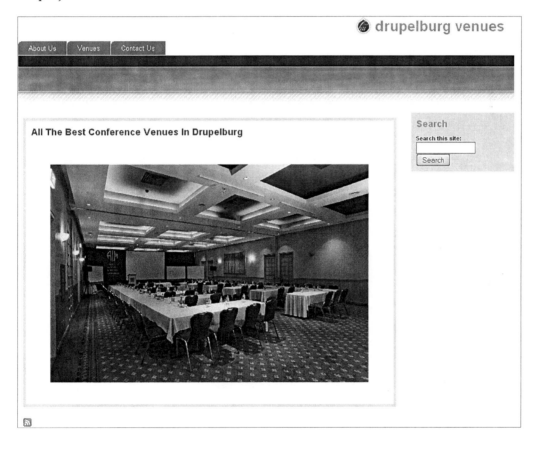

# Summary

In this chapter, you learned how to:

- Build a basic site for listing bookable items by using the **Availability Calendar** module

- Add the Fivestar rating widgets to nodes

- Use the **SimpleViews** and **Views** modules to quickly create useful content views

# 11
# Alienspotting—Building a Google Map Site

When Winston Groovy returned home to his wife Rita in Kingston, Jamaica, after being missing for two days, Rita was not amused. This was the third weekend in a row that Winston had claimed to have been abducted by aliens. But Winston really did seem quite sincere and sober ("Yeah man! dem mash me up", he claimed), and Rita was, as usual, very forgiving and quite happy to have her Winston back home. However, to save other people from the heartache of having their loved ones permanently lost to extra-terrestrial kidnappers, Rita Groovy has decided to create a web site called Alienspotting to aggregate occurrences of alien sightings all over the world. The web site will consist of:

- A description of encounters with aliens, including photos, if available
- A means for the site users to comment on stories, with recent comments being shown in a side bar
- A front page world map, with each documented encounter appearing on this map as a marker

# Theme

Alienspotting will use the "Fervens" theme, which is a contribution to the Drupal project.

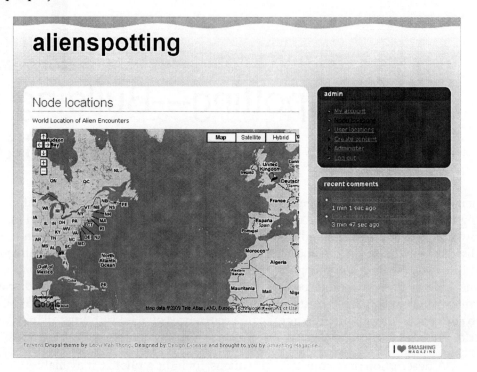

# Build Alienspotting

In order to create this web site, we need to do the following:

- Configure the **GMap** module to display nodes on a map
- Configure the node type to be used with **GMap**
- Permit nodes to be commented on
- Put the most recent comments in a sidebar block

# Modules

Alienspotting is built around the **GMap** module, and can be surprisingly easy to build. For this web site, we will be using the following modules:

## Optional Core modules

We will be enabling and using the following **Core** modules:

- **Comment** – permits users to comment on stories
- **Upload** – allows the upload of files and images into content

## Contributed modules

We will also upload and enable the following contributed modules:

- **GMap** – allows the insertion of a Google map into a node.
- **Location** – allows you to associate a geographic location with content and users.
- **CCK** – allows the easy creation of new content fields. This module is necessary for the **Location** module.
- **Image** – allows users with the correct permissions to upload images. Thumbnails and additional sizes are created automatically.

## Enable modules

First visit the **Modules** page, and enable all of the modules that are required. You may not need all of the modules under **GMap**, but select them all anyway, if you are unsure of how much modification you intend to make to this, our basic design. Under **Location**, select **Location** and **Node Locations**. Under **CCK**, you must select **Content** and **Location CCK**.

# Configure GMap

We need to configure the **GMap** module before it can function. For this, visit the link for the **GMap** module on the **Administer** page, and there we will see a page similar to the one shown in the following screenshot:

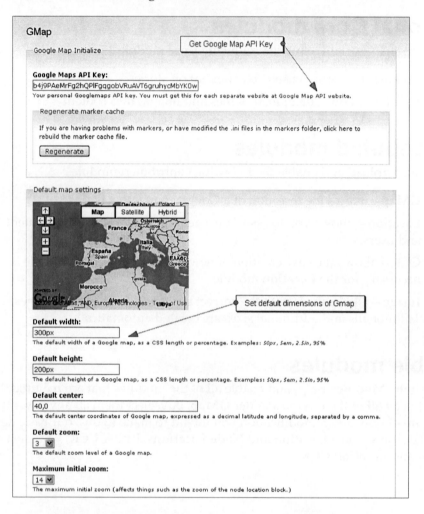

The most important task on this page is to obtain the **Google Map API Key**. The module will not function without it. The API key is site-specific and can be obtained from the Google API site. The API key may also have Terms and Conditions notices and usage limits. A link to the site is provided on this GMap configuration page. Follow this link, and observe all of the instructions that the Google Maps site gives you, in order to acquire an API key. After this, return to the configuration page, and paste the API key into the box where it is required.

If you want to change the display dimension(s) of the Google map, for example if it will be used in a node view, then you can also change it on this page. Otherwise, just leave all of the other settings with their default values, and then save the page.

# GMap Location

In the **GMap Location** link on the **Administer** page, we will be able to configure two views: the user map and the node map. The user map should show a map with all of the registered site users who have supplied their location details, while the node map will enable a map showing the location of all of the nodes on the site. We will only concern ourselves with the node map at this time, because all that Rita Groovy wants to be shown on the map are the locations of reported alien sightings.

Go to the **GMap Location** settings page. In the **Node Map** setting section, near the bottom end of the page, alter the settings for **Page header**, and also define the actions to be performed when the marker is clicked on, along with the appearance of the markers. In this case, we have changed the **Page header** to **World Location of Alien Encounters**. We have also set markers to show the associated node when it is clicked on, and we have determined that all of our markers will be of a **Small Red** type.

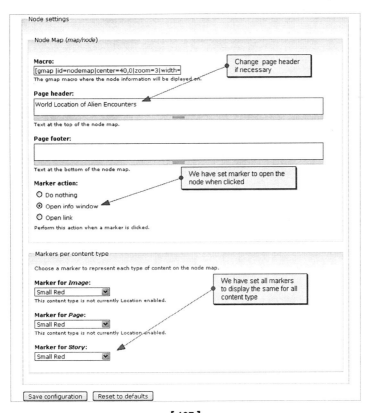

# Configure Location

The **Location** module may also need to be configured, even though it will work with the default settings. Access the configuration page for **Location** on the **Administer** page, and this will show the following view for the **Main settings**:

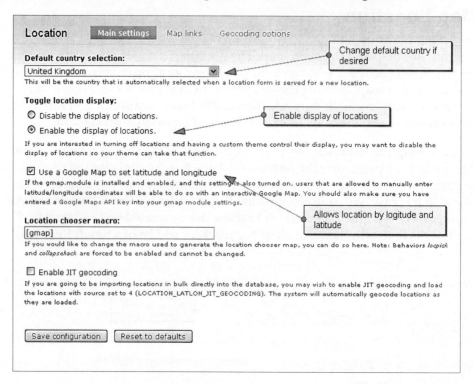

The other settings located in the **Map links** and **Geocoding options** windows are optional for this exercise, so we shall be leaving them with their default values.

# Basic content

The primary content for this web site will be reports of Alien sightings, which are submitted by users from all over the world. This part will be handled by the **Story** Content type. An extra section is to be made available in the submission form for this Content type, to allow users to add their location. It is from this location that a marker will be placed on the GMap to identify the node with the location.

# Configure the Story Content type

By going to the **Administer** page of the site and then to the **Content management** section, we will find the **Content types** link.

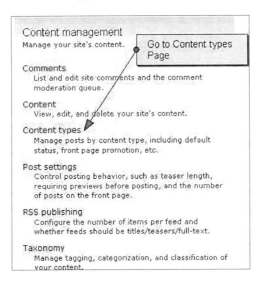

If we access this link, then we will see the various Content types listed. We will not be creating any new Content types.

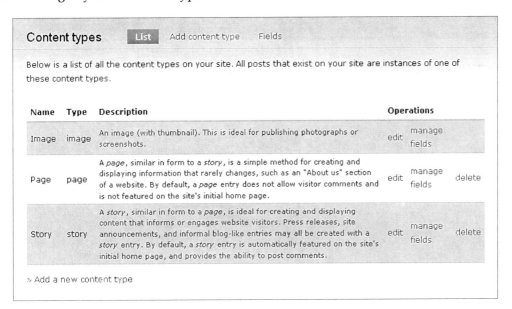

However, we will be configuring the **Story** Content type for our purposes:

1.  Click on the **edit** link of the **Story** Content type; you will be presented with a form.

2.  In the **Workflow settings**, we need to determine the default options:

    ° Do you want the story to be published and made available on the site immediately after submission? If so, select the **Published** checkbox.

    ° Do you want the story promoted to the front page? If so, select the **Promoted to front page** checkbox.

    ° Do you want the story to remain at the top of the list of contents on the site? If so, select the **Sticky at top of list** checkbox.

3.  In the **Comments settings**, indicate whether you want to allow comments to be made for the nodes or not, and if you do, then how these comments will be handled.

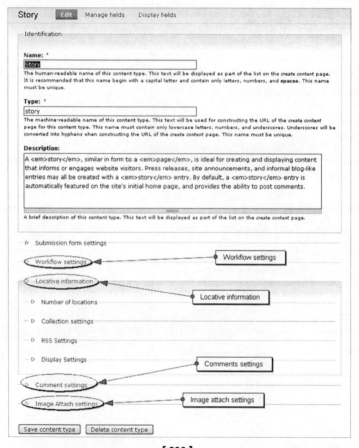

Perhaps the most important settings are the individual nodes' **Locative information** (for the number of locations), collection settings, and the display settings.

# Number of locations

For the settings in the **Number of locations**, we have given the following values:

- **Minimum number of locations** = 1; because the node must have a location

- **Maximum number of locations** = 1; because the node must have no more than one location

- **Number of locations that can be added at once** = 1; because only one location is allowed

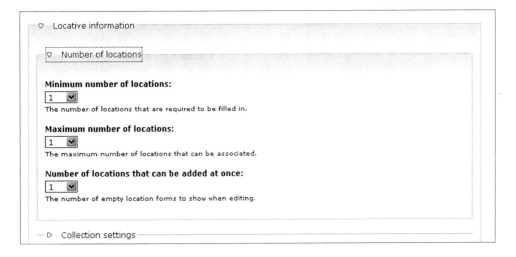

# Collection settings

In the **Collection settings**, we define how the location information will be entered, what the form will look like, and what fields will be used, as shown in the following screenshot:

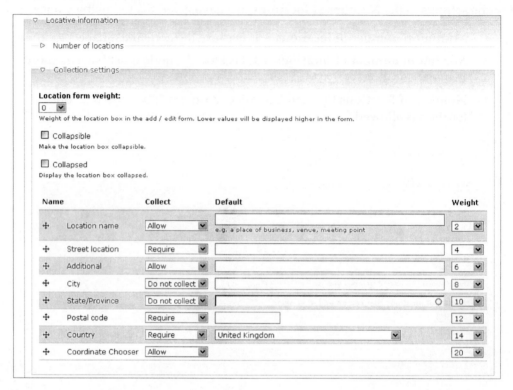

We have deselected the **Collapsible** and **Collapsed** checkboxes to ensure that the location form always remains visible and is not collapsed.

We have also decided which fields should be presented in the form. In this context, the form fields can be interpreted as follows:

- **Allow** — the field value is allowed to be submitted
- **Require** — the field value MUST be submitted
- **Do not collect** — the field will be omitted

# Display settings

Finally, the **Display Settings** specify where the location will be shown, and what fields will be shown. The selectable values are self-descriptive, as shown in the following screenshot:

# Images

At the bottom of the form for this Content type, you will see a panel for **Image Attach settings**. Enable **Attach image**, and now the Alienspotting users will be able to post pictures of UFOs and spacemen. In order to confirm this, go to the **Create content** link for the **Story** Content type. Near the bottom end of the page, you will find the **Attached images** panel, where the users can upload images of their alien sightings.

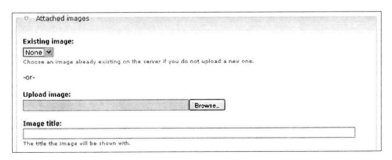

# Test the Story submission form

Now let us test our **Story** submission form, and see how it works. In order to do this, click on the **Create content** link on the lefthand side of your page, and select **Story**. You will see a form, similar to the one shown in the following screenshot:

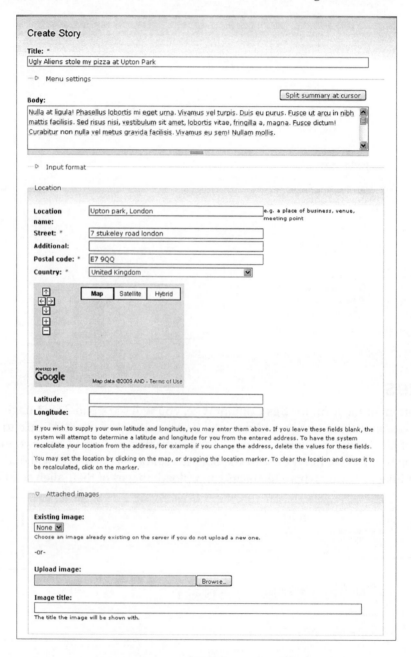

Post some stories to make sure that your site has been set up correctly. You should end up with a typical page, similar to the one shown in the following screenshot:

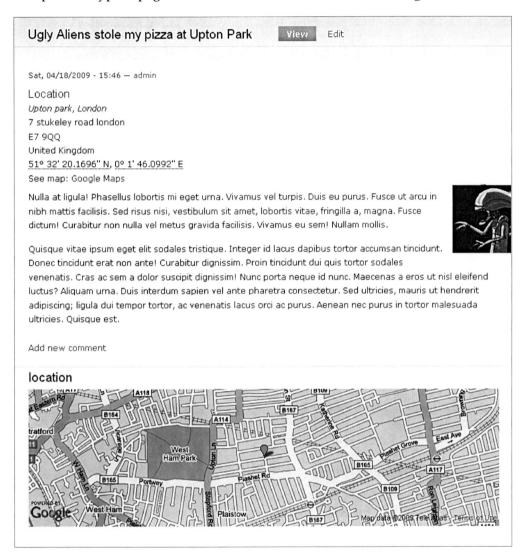

# Display content

Now, what this site is specifically set up to do is to display all of the alien encounters as node locations on a Google map.

# Node locations

Under the **admin** menu on the side bar, we will find a link for **Node locations**. If we click on this, then we will be presented with a page containing a map that shows all of the nodes as markers (like in the following screenshot). If we click on any single marker, then we will be shown the content of the node represented by the marker.

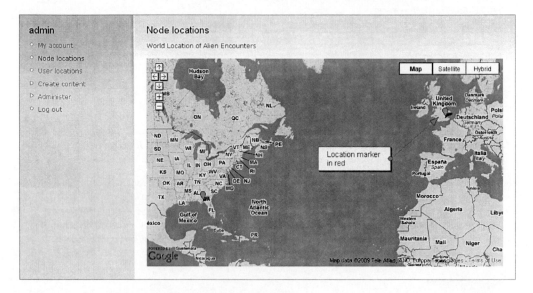

However, what we actually want is to have this map displayed on the front page. Therefore, we will go the **Site information** link on the **Administer** page, and at the bottom of the page, set the **Default front page** to **map/node**, which is the URL of the node location map.

# Recent comments

When configuring our **Story** Content type for use, we would have selected that comments are permitted for this Content type. In order to decide which user roles will be permitted to post comments, we can access the **Access control** link on the **Administer** page.

Again, we go to the **Blocks** page, and there we will find the **Recent comments** block, which we will move to the **Right sidebar**, which is where we want it.

# Finishing up

We can now enable our new theme, **Fervens**, on the **Themes** page, and we have given Rita Groovy some hints about the places to go looking if Winston permanently disappears.

# Summary

In this chapter, you have learned how to:

- Build a basic site based on the **GMap** module
- Use the **GMap** module to create a typical Google map mashup

# 12
# Weird Hap'nins—Building a News Aggregating Site

Bad news is always good news for the press. This is why Vaughan Pyre has decided to take advantage of this fact and create a web site that will aggregate bad news and weird happenings from all over the world. The content of the site will be entirely derived from **Really Simple Syndication (RSS)** feeds from several sources (each feed being automatically fetched and its items displayed on the web site).

Weird Hap'nins requirements will be the need to:

- Get external feed sources and allocate them to menu links on the web site
- Create the means to automatically fetch and display article items located in the feeds
- Display blocks of latest content from each feed source on the front page

# Theme

The theme chosen is "Strange Little Town", which is a contributed theme that fits the description of this unique web site.

# Build Weird Hap'nins

Vaughan Pyre is a very ambitious webpreneur. What he really hopes for is a web site that is completely self-maintaining, and on which he can place some **Google AdSense** blocks. Clicks from the visitors to his site will ensure that he makes lots of money. For this, he needs a site where the content updates regularly with fresh content so that visitors will keep coming back to click on some more Google ads. Vaughan's ultimate objective is to create several of these web sites.

# Modules

This is, surprisingly, a very simple site to build, and much of the requirements can be achieved by using the Core **Aggregator** module. Indeed, were it not for the fact that Vaughan needs the content to automatically update, we needn't use any module other than the **Aggregator** module.

## Optional Core modules

We will be using the following **Core** modules, which can be enabled via the **Modules** page:

- **Aggregator** — for aggregating syndicated content (RSS, RDF, and Atom feeds)

## Contributed modules

We will also be using the following contributed modules from `Drupal.org`. Install, and enable them via the **Modules** page:

- **Poormanscron** — internal scheduler for users without a cron application

## Configure the Poormanscron module

First we need to enable the **Poormanscron** module, so that the incoming feeds will be able to self-refresh. From the **Administer** page, we will access the **Poormanscron** configuration page, mainly to set the time interval between runs of cron to update feed items, as shown in the following screenshot:

In this case, we have left the **Time intervals** at the default value of **60** minutes.

# Configure the Aggregator module

The **Aggregator** module should be configured to define the feed sources, how often they will be polled, and how they're categorized. For this, if we select the **Feed aggregator** link on the **Administer** page, then we should arrive at the following page:

| Feed aggregator | List | Add category | Add feed | Settings |

Thousands of sites (particularly news sites and blogs) publish their latest headlines and posts in feeds, using a number of standardized XML-based formats. Formats supported by the aggregator include RSS, RDF, and Atom.

Current feeds are listed below, and new feeds may be added. For each feed or feed category, the *latest items* block may be enabled at the blocks administration page.

[more help...]

Feed overview

| Title | Items | Last update | Next update | Operations |
| --- | --- | --- | --- | --- |

Category overview

| Title | Items | Operations |
| --- | --- | --- |

On the **Settings** page, we will define some more requirements, as follows:

1. **Allowed HTML tags** — which are the tags that are embedded in the incoming feed that we want Drupal to accept. The allowed tags do not include image tags. So if any images are coming with the feed, then they will be excluded. However, we don't want this to happen, so we have added the image tag `<img>` to the list.

2. **Items shown in sources and categories pages** — we have defined this to be **20 items**, but you may select another figure.

3. **Discard items older than** — we want the feed items to be completely refreshed every week so we have set this at **1 week.**

4. **Category selection type** — we are not categorizing the feeds, so we will leave this setting as it is.

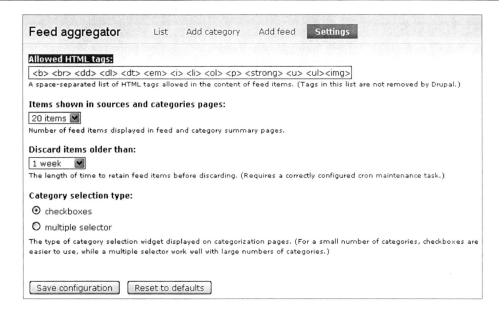

# Basic content

The site is built around the **Aggregator** module, and no other Content type will need to be created. Vaughan has decided to initially use three feeds obtained from `www.newsfeedmaker.com`, as follows:

- **Bad News** — `http://www.newsfeedmaker.com/feed.php?code=ddb874f7`
- **Crime** — `http://www.newsfeedmaker.com/feed.php?code=33a5a46a`
- **Paranormal** — `http://www.newsfeedmaker.com/feed.php?code=936f006a`

It is from these feeds that we will create the necessary content.

**Tips and traps**

An excellent source for "mashup" feeds on any topic is `pipes.yahoo.com`.

# Add feeds

On the **Add feeds** page, which is under the **Feed aggregator** configuration page, we finally get to define our feeds, and how often we want them to be polled.

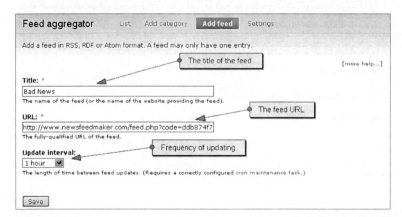

We want our **Bad News** feed to be polled every hour, so we have configured it this way. The same procedure is followed to create the feeds for **Crime** and **Paranormal**.

# Display the feeds

It is necessary to first start the feeds so that you can be sure that they work. Therefore, if we go to the **List** tab on the **Feed aggregator** page and click on the **update items** link on the righthand side of each listed feed, then we will see that the site polls items from the feeds that we have configured.

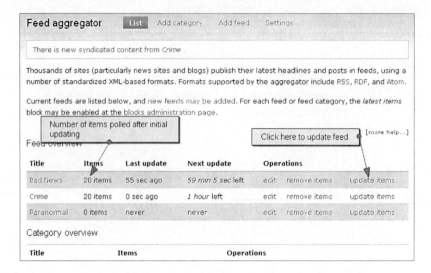

Clicking on the **Title** of the feed on this page will show a page view of the resulting feed. For example, the **Bad News** page gives us the following view:

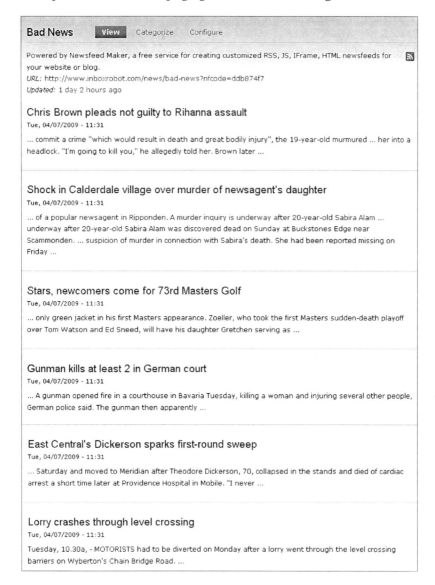

# Newsfeed blocks

Vaughan wants to have blocks containing the latest items from the incoming feeds placed on the front page to encourage visitors to read more and to visit more often. If we visit the **Blocks** page, then we will see that blocks for **Bad News feed latest items**, **Crime feed latest items**, and **Paranormal feed latest items** have been conveniently created by the **Aggregator** module. We may now assign these blocks to the **Bottom Content** region, and configure the blocks to only show on the front page.

# Create the front page post

Vaughan needs only one post on the front page, and wants this to be placed at the top of the page, to describe the web site. This post will be created from the **Page** Content type. In order to do this, click on the **Create content** link on the lefthand side of the screen, and select the **Page** link. You will see a form similar to the one shown in the following screenshot:

In this form, we enter the introductory text for the site. At the bottom of the page, in the **Publishing option** panel, we will promote it to the front page and make it **Sticky at top of list**. This is necessary just in case Vaughan decides to add new items to the front page, which may effectively displace the site description post that he always wants to be at the top.

**Tips and traps**

Remember to change the permissions to **access news feeds** on the **Administer | User management | Permissions** page.

# Menus

Now let's tidy up our site by creating a menu system that is more intuitive. For simplicity, we will be putting all of our feeds page views menu under a new **Feeds** menu, to separate it from our user's menu.

In order to do this, go to the **Menu** link on the **Administer** page.

1. Click on the **Add menu** tab at the top of this page to access the page that will permit you to add the new menu (in our example the **Feeds** menu), as shown in the following screenshot:

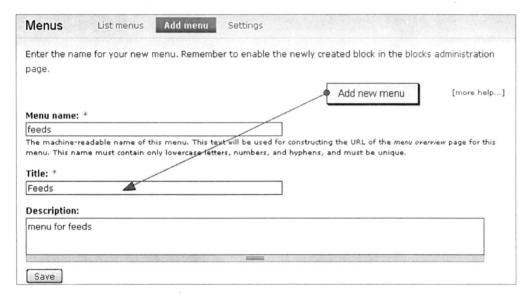

2. After this, we need to create the menu items that link to each of the feeds pages. The URLs for the feeds that we have created are:
   - **Bad News** — aggregator/sources/1
   - **Crime** — aggregator/sources/2

   °   **Paranormal** — `aggregator/sources/3`

These URLs may be obtained from the display in the browser without the preceding string (`http://.../?q=`).

Return to the **Menus** link on the **Administer** page and select **Feeds**. At the top of the page that comes up, select the **Add item** tab. This will take us to a page (shown in the following screenshot) where we can define the items in our menu.

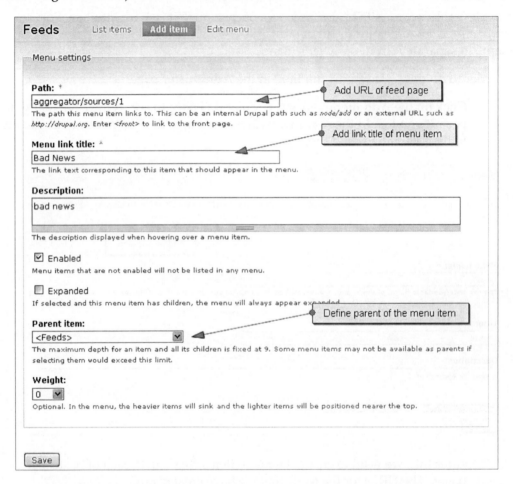

We will also see from the **Blocks** link on the **Administer** page that a new block has been created for **Feeds**, and we will assign this to the **Right sidebar**, which is where we want it.

# Finishing up

We can now enable our new theme, **Strange Little Town**, on the **Themes** page, which will give us a new front page, as shown in the following screenshot:

# Summary

In this chapter, you have learned how to:

- Build a basic site for publishing news feeds, using the **Aggregator** module
- Use the **Poormanscron** module to run regular site tasks

# Installation and Configuration

Like every other endeavor in life, there are two ways of installing Drupal—the easy way and the difficult way. In order to do it the difficult way, you will need to set up your server by yourself before you proceed with the installation. You have the choice of environment to use for your new install: you may install directly to a live server, or you can set up a test environment on your local computer.

## Install on a local computer

There are a number of ways to set up a test environment on your own local computer. Most time-pressed developers will install and configure directly onto a live server, but there are good reasons for running your application first on a local development server:

- Developing locally allows you to work when you are not online.

- Getting your local server running, even if it is with a simple installation like **WampServer** for a machine running Windows or **MAMP** for a Mac, it will help you to start thinking in terms of server processes and databases. As you get deeper into Drupal, this knowledge will pay off.

- Everything that you put on the web is searched, archived, and hangs around for quite a bit of time. We certainly don't want our inevitable learning mistakes to be displayed for the world to see via Google.

# Installation on Wampserver

**WampServer2** enables us to run Apache, MySQL, and PHP on Windows and is available for free. You can download it from http://www.wampserver.com.

The WampServer2 package comes with the following components already configured to work together:

- Apache 2.2.11
- MySQL 5.1.30
- PHP 5.2.8

There are similar packages that already include Drupal (such as DeveloperSide and WDE). However, note that these may not always have the latest secure version of Drupal. Therefore, it is better to use WampServer2, and load it with the Drupal version of your choice. Acquia also has a bundled application that may be obtained from the web site `http://acquia.com`.

WampServer2 is self-installing. Just double-click on the icon after you've unpacked your zipped download, and follow the installation instructions. This gets your development environment ready in just a few minutes. Now let the fun begin!

# Install Drupal 6 on localhost

Installing Drupal on localhost can be remarkably straightforward:

1. Download the latest stable release of Drupal, and unzip it until it gives you a discernible `Drupal X.X` folder. You will need to use a tool like Winzip for Windows (`http://www.winzip.com`) to do this.

2. Locate the directory in which WampServer2 is installed on your computer. This will usually be the root of your computer's main directory (usually `C:\`) and in a folder named `Wamp`. Open it; find the `www` folder and copy your `Drupal X.X` folder into it. Name the Drupal folder as per your preference. In the unlikely scenario that you will be installing only one Drupal test site on your local machine, you may — just for the sake of having a longer life — name it Drupal.

3. Go to your computer desktop taskbar tray, click on the WampServer icon, and select the **Start all services** option (if this has not yet been selected).

4. Now open your browser, and navigate to `http://localhost`. This will bring up the main WampServer2 interface, and you will see your project, Drupal, under **Your Projects**.

5.  However, because Drupal needs a database to run, we must create the database for our project. Click on the **phpMyAdmin** link. This will bring up another interface, this time for phpMyAdmin. Enter the name of your new database in the **Create new database** Field. For the simple reason that we shouldn't live a complicated life, we have given this database the same name (**Drupal**) as our project and as our install folder. We are now ready to install Drupal.

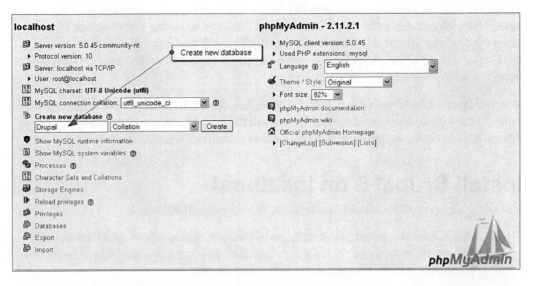

6.  Locate the file `default.settings.php` in the **Drupal | sites | default** folder, and rename this file to `settings.php`. Make sure that the write permission for this file has been enabled.

7.  Drupal has an automated installation script that automatically populates database tables and sets the correct settings in the `settings.php` file. The install script will set the base URL, connect Drupal to the database, and create tables in the database. Navigate to `http://localhost/Drupal`, and start your installation.

8.  You will be presented with a step-by-step guide to the installation. After correcting any host-specific errors, you will be taken to the **Database configuration** page.

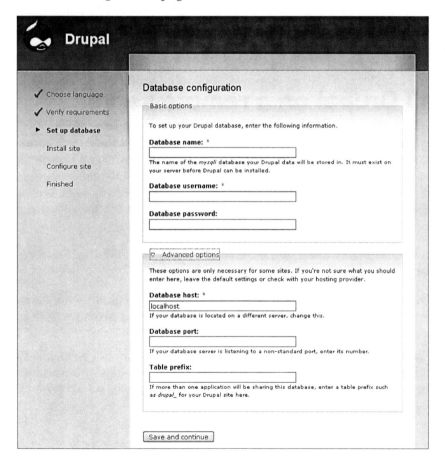

9. Add the following required parameters on the page:
   - ° **Database name**: **Experience** (or whatever you have called yours).
   - ° **Database User name**: **root** (unless you have changed it).
   - ° **Database Password**: Leave blank (unless you have added one when you set up your database).
   - ° **Database host**: **localhost**.
   - ° **Database port**: Ignore this.
   - ° **Table prefix**: If you are installing more than one instance of Drupal in a single database, then give one of them a prefix (such as **DR2_**), or else the second instance will not install. Otherwise, you may safely ignore this.

Next, click on **Save and continue**. In a few seconds or so, your installation success screen will be displayed, along with a title **Configure site**. Congratulations, you are now on your way to becoming a Drupal Guru!

# Install Drupal on a remote server

The steps for performing this installation are essentially the same as for installing Drupal on a local machine. Some other hosting packages will come with one-click installation tools such as **Fantastico**—a commercial script library that automates the installation of web applications to a web site. Fantastico scripts are executed from the administration area of a website's control panel, such as CPanel. The scripts typically create tables in a database, install the software, adjust permissions, and modify the web server's configuration files.

Although they may look like a god send, hosting providers offering Fantastico do have several minuses:

- The installation scripts, although easy to use, are frequently not maintained by the hosting companies, and thus older releases of products with known security problems are in current use.
- The default configuration for many applications may not be secure. So, although the systems are easy to set up, it also provides opportunities, for example, for spammers to write automated scripts, which post spam messages on web sites.

- Some hosting companies, in their eagerness to improve the user experience and heighten security, like to share an update as soon as a new release is available. However, Drupal add-ons tend to not be backward compatible across versions. Advanced Drupal users know that it may be wise to wait until a new release supports the functionality, that their web site requires, before adopting it for use.

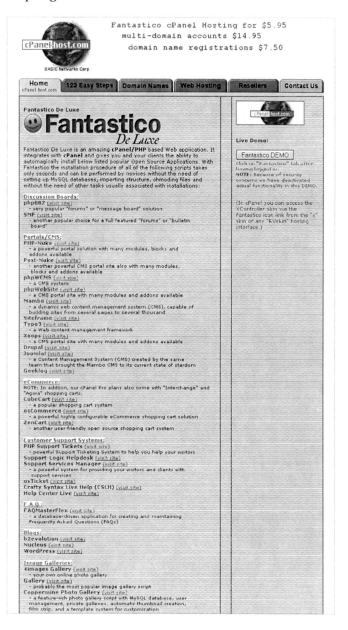

# Other installation possibilities

Installing Drupal on a remote server without Fantastico is quite similar to the localhost procedure. The method of creating a database varies greatly across hosting companies, and you are advised to contact the hosting company if there is any confusion as to how to go about doing this.

In order to install Drupal on a non-Windows localhost, and for troubleshooting the installation, adequate documentation exists on the project website http://drupal. org, where an active forum exists with answers to every problem that may be encountered during installation.

# Configuration and backend administration

Once the install script has successfully completed, you will be directed to the **Configure site** page. This page outlines, in brief, the basic steps required to set up and configure your Drupal site. Take a moment to review them.

On completion of the installation, you will generally be presented with two errors—one indicating that cron is not configured, and the other regarding the file system. Configuring cron will be done later. For now, click on the **run cron manually** link to clear the error.

The files directory is where all of the uploaded content is stored. If you use CSS aggregation, then it stores those files there as well. You can follow one of two procedures:

- Create it yourself at the root directory of your site
- Click on the link in the **File system** settings page, and Drupal will attempt to create the files directory automatically

In most configurations, automatic creation will be fine.

## Site information

From the **Site information** link, you are able to do some basic personalization of your site and change some basic information. For example, you may want to change the name of the site from **Drupal** to a name of your choice, as well as change other basic parameters and information.

## Site information

**Name:** *

[                                        ]

The name of this website.

**E-mail address:** *

[                                        ]

The *From* address in automated e-mails sent during registration and new password requests, and other notifications. (Use an address ending in your site's domain to help prevent this e-mail being flagged as spam.)

**Slogan:**

[                                        ]

Your site's motto, tag line, or catchphrase (often displayed alongside the title of the site).

**Mission:**

[                                                            ]

Your site's mission or focus statement (often prominently displayed on the front page).

**Footer message:**

[                                                            ]

This text will be displayed at the bottom of each page. Useful for adding a copyright notice to your pages.

**Anonymous user:** *

[Anonymous                              ]

The name used to indicate anonymous users.

**Default front page:** *

http://localhost/alien/?q= [node                    ]

The home page displays content from this relative URL. If unsure, specify "node".

[ Save configuration ]   [ Reset to defaults ]

Here is a list of things that you may easily do here:

- Set the **Name** of your site.
- Set the **E-mail address** for your site (for outgoing only **noreply@sample.com** works).
- Set a **Slogan** for your site, if you want.
- The **Mission** statement is optional. The mission statement is available to some themes and only displays on the front page when this feature is enabled.
- Define a **Footer** message can be displayed if you need one.
- Define a default name for an **Anonymous user**, if you allow anonymous user posting.
- **Default front page** — by default, this is set to **node**. When set to **node**, this displays, in order, all of the posts with **Promote to front page** selected. You can set it to a specific node for a static front page (such as `node/4`).

# Theme settings

You may also change your default theme by visiting the **Themes** link on the **Administer** page.

In a new install, **Garland** is enabled as the default theme. Select another theme from the list if you don't feel comfortable with the default theme, or if you have uploaded your own theme into the `themes` folder.

You may also want to change how the content is displayed by the theme. Click on the **Global settings** link for the themes, and take a look at the other options available here. You may also upload your own custom 'favicon' to replace the smiling Druplicon.

New themes, and help on using and configuring them, can be found on the project web site at `http://drupal.org`.

# B
# Optimizing your Site

When a user performs a task on your Drupal site, a query is sent to the database. If it is for a page request, then all of the raw data needed to display this page is retrieved from the database. The browser then attempts to put the data together with all of the other elements of the page such as the CSS code, JavaScript, images, Flash, and other objects. The speed with which your requested page loads will be constrained by server efficiency, Internet connection, and also the size of the individual components of the page that are being assembled. Heavy files, such as Flash, video, and large images, could take quite a bit of time to load, especially over a slow connection.

Thankfully, there are some native Drupal settings and optimization techniques that can improve the browsing experience of your site user. Consider the following scenarios:

- Your site has more than just a few modules installed. Many of these modules will typically have their own CSS and JavaScript files, and so the browser is given the unenviable task of first fetching these individual files from wherever they may be and then properly interpreting them before serving the page to the user.

- Your site has heavy traffic and each user is making requests of the database at the same time as the others. The database is, however, not limitless; it is like a machine, and what happens to a machine that is put under too much stress is that it eventually breaks down.

Drupal is able to reduce the load on database and to store cached pages that have been previously requested by other users. When these pages are requested again, they are simply passed on to the user from the cache, without the need for making multiple requests from the database. However, the caching feature is disabled by default, primarily because it could affect other configuration. In order to access this feature and the other core functionalities that may be used to improve the performance of the Drupal site, we will need to find the **Performance** link on the **Administer** page, which will take us to the page shown in the following screenshot:

## Performance

### Page cache

Enabling the page cache will offer a significant performance boost. Drupal can store and send compressed cached pages requested by *anonymous* users. By caching a web page, Drupal does not have to construct the page each time it is viewed.

**Caching mode:**

⦿ Disabled

○ Normal (recommended for production sites, no side effects)

○ Aggressive (experts only, possible side effects)

The normal cache mode is suitable for most sites and does not cause any side effects. The aggressive cache mode causes Drupal to skip the loading (boot) and unloading (exit) of enabled modules when serving a cached page. This results in an additional performance boost but can cause unwanted side effects.

The following enabled modules are incompatible with aggressive mode caching and will not function properly: *uc_cart, uc_store*.

**Minimum cache lifetime:**

| <none> ▾ |

On high-traffic sites, it may be necessary to enforce a minimum cache lifetime. The minimum cache lifetime is the minimum amount of time that will elapse before the cache is emptied and recreated, and is applied to both page and block caches. A larger minimum cache lifetime offers better performance, but users will not see new content for a longer period of time.

**Page compression:**

○ Disabled

⦿ Enabled

By default, Drupal compresses the pages it caches in order to save bandwidth and improve download times. This option should be disabled when using a webserver that performs compression.

### Block cache

Enabling the block cache can offer a performance increase for all users by preventing blocks from being reconstructed on each page load. If the page cache is also enabled, performance increases from enabling the block cache will mainly benefit authenticated users.

**Block cache:**

⦿ Disabled

○ Enabled (recommended)

Note that block caching is inactive when modules defining content access restrictions are enabled.

### Bandwidth optimizations

Drupal can automatically optimize external resources like CSS and JavaScript, which can reduce both the size and number of requests made to your website. CSS files can be aggregated and compressed into a single file, while JavaScript files are aggregated (but not compressed). These optional optimizations may reduce server load, bandwidth requirements, and page loading times.

These options are disabled if you have not set up your files directory, or if your download method is set to private.

**Optimize CSS files:**

⦿ Disabled

○ Enabled

This option can interfere with theme development and should only be enabled in a production environment.

**Optimize JavaScript files:**

⦿ Disabled

○ Enabled

This option can interfere with module development and should only be enabled in a production environment.

### Clear cached data

Caching data improves performance, but may cause problems while troubleshooting new modules, themes, or translations, if outdated information has been cached. To refresh all cached data on your site, click the button below. *Warning: high-traffic sites will experience performance slowdowns while cached data is rebuilt.*

[ Clear cached data ]

[ Save configuration ]  [ Reset to defaults ]

Here is what you may do on this page.

# Page cache

Enabling the page cache will offer a significant performance boost. Drupal can store and send compressed cached pages requested by anonymous users. By caching a web page, Drupal does not have to construct the page each time it is viewed.

The **Normal** cache mode is suitable for most sites and does not cause any side effects. The **Aggressive** cache mode causes Drupal to skip the loading (boot) and unloading (exit) of enabled modules when serving a cached page. This results in an additional performance boost but can cause unwanted side effects and may actually be incompatible with some modules.

# Minimum cache lifetime

On high-traffic sites, it may be necessary to enforce a **Minimum cache lifetime**. The **Minimum cache lifetime** is the minimum amount of time that will elapse before the cache is emptied and recreated, and is applied to both page and block caches. A larger **Minimum cache lifetime** offers better performance, but users will not see new content for a longer period of time.

# Page compression

By default, Drupal compresses the pages that it caches in order to save bandwidth and improve download times. This option should be disabled when using a web server that performs compression.

# Block cache

Enabling the **Block cache** can offer a performance increase for all of the users by preventing blocks from being reconstructed on each page load. If the page cache is also enabled, then the performance increase from enabling the block cache will mainly benefit authenticated users. Note that block caching is inactive when modules that define content access restrictions are enabled.

# Bandwidth optimizations

Drupal can automatically optimize external resources, such as CSS and JavaScript, which can reduce both the size and the number of requests made to your web site. CSS files can be aggregated and compressed into a single file, while JavaScript files are aggregated (but not compressed). These optional optimizations may reduce server load, bandwidth requirements, and page loading times.

These options are disabled if you have not set up your files directory, or if your download method is set to private.

## Optimize CSS files

This option can interfere with theme development and should only be enabled in a production environment. If you are making changes to the CSS of your theme and these changes don't seem to be having any effect, then turn this option off.

## Optimize JavaScript files

This option can interfere with module development and should only be enabled in a production environment. It also breaks some libraries, like TinyMCE, which cannot be compressed.

## Clear cached data

Caching data improves performance, but it may also cause problems while troubleshooting new modules, themes, or translations, if outdated information has been cached.

# Other optimization techniques

There are a few other optimization techniques possible, but for the normal Drupal site with low to average traffic, the foregoing techniques should suffice to improve performance. However, when traffic begins to get a bit out of hand, you can engage some other modules. The **Throttle**, **Boost**, and **Advanced cache** modules have proved to be very popular for a normal site residing on a shared server.

# Throttle

The core distribution of Drupal includes a module called **Throttle**. In order to reduce server load, modules with their **Throttle** checkbox selected are temporarily disabled when the site becomes extremely busy. The **Throttle** checkbox is only available if the **Throttle** module is enabled. What the **Throttle** module does is it measures the site load by sampling the number of current users and by turning off functionality, if the sampling indicates that the threshold set by the administrator has been reached. It may be wise to turn this module on when the site is being configured.

# Boost

What Drupal's built-in caching does is cut down on the code that needs to run on each page request, while reducing the database access to a single query that retrieves the cached page to display. This in itself provides a marked speed-up, sure enough, but still necessitates invoking PHP on each page request, and what's worse opens a connection to the backend database. These connections become a scarce resource once the going gets tough. In contrast, the **Boost** module exports Drupal pages into static HTML files. When a page request can be satisfied from the static cache, PHP is bypassed in its entirety, and the web server serves the cached file directly from the disk at the top speed that it is capable of.

# Advanced cache

The **Advanced caching** module is mostly a set of patches and a supporting  module that brings caching to the Drupal core in places where it is needed, yet is currently unavailable. These include caching nodes, comments, taxonomy, path aliases, and search results.

# C
# Themes and Modules

## CHAPTER 1

|  | VERSION | PROJECT PAGE |
|---|---|---|
| **THEME** | | |
| AD The Morning After | 6.x-1.5 | http://drupal.org/project/ad_the-morning-after |
| **CONTRIBUTED MODULES** | | |
| Taxonomy Menu | 6.x-1.02 | http://drupal.org/project/taxonomy_menu |
| IMCE | 6.x-1.2 | http://drupal.org/project/imce |
| Image | 6.x-1.0 | http://drupal.org/project/image |

## CHAPTER 2

|  | VERSION | PROJECT PAGE |
|---|---|---|
| **THEME** | | |
| Beginning | 6.x-1.4 | http://drupal.org/project/beginning |
| **CONTRIBUTED MODULES** | | |
| Webform | 6.x-2.7 | http://drupal.org/project/webform |
| Views | 6.x-2.6 | http://drupal.org/project/views |
| SimpleViews | 6.x-1.0 | http://drupal.org/project/simpleviews |
| Image | 6.x-1.0 | http://drupal.org/project/image |
| IMCE | 6.x-1.2 | http://drupal.org/project/imce |
| Taxonomy Menu | 6.x-1.02 | http://drupal.org/project/taxonomy_menu |
| TinyMCE | 6.x-1.1 | http://drupal.org/project/tinymce |

## CHAPTER 3

|  | VERSION | PROJECT PAGE |
|---|---|---|
| **THEME** | | |
| Pushbutton | core | |
| **CONTRIBUTED MODULES** | | |
| Taxonomy Menu | 6.x-1.02 | http://drupal.org/project/taxonomy_menu |
| IMCE | 6.x-1.2 | http://drupal.org/project/imce |
| Image | 6.x-1.0 | http://drupal.org/project/image |
| TinyMCE | 6.x-1.1 | http://drupal.org/project/tinymce |

## CHAPTER 4

|  | VERSION | PROJECT PAGE |
|---|---|---|
| **THEME** | | |
| Terrafirma | 6.x-2.1 | http://drupal.org/project/terrafirma_theme |
| **CONTRIBUTED MODULES** | | |
| Event | 6.x-2.x | http://drupal.org/project/event |
| Notify | 6.x-1.0 | http://drupal.org/project/notify |
| Signup | 6.x-1.0-rc3 | http://drupal.org/project/signup |
| Image | 6.x-1.0 | http://drupal.org/project/image |
| IMCE | 6.x-1.2 | http://drupal.org/project/imce |
| Taxonomy Menu | 6.x-1.02 | http://drupal.org/project/taxonomy_menu |
| TinyMCE | 6.x-1.1 | http://drupal.org/project/tinymce |

## CHAPTER 5

|  | VERSION | PROJECT PAGE |
|---|---|---|
| **THEME** | | |
| Multiflex-3 | 6.x-1.5 | `http://drupal.org/project/multiflex3` |
| **CONTRIBUTED MODULES** | | |
| OG | 6.x-1.3 | `http://drupal.org/project/og` |
| Tribune | 6.x-1.10 | `http://drupal.org/project/tribune` |
| Image | 6.x-1.0 | `http://drupal.org/project/image` |
| IMCE | 6.x-1.2 | `http://drupal.org/project/imce` |

## CHAPTER 6

|  | VERSION | PROJECT PAGE |
|---|---|---|
| **THEME** | | |
| Analytic | 6.x-1.3 | `http://drupal.org/project/analytic` |
| **CONTRIBUTED MODULES** | | |
| Image | 6.x-1.0 | `http://drupal.org/project/image` |
| IMCE | 6.x-1.2 | `http://drupal.org/project/imce` |
| Panels | 6.x-2.0 | `http://drupal.org/project/panels` |
| Views | 6.x-2.6 | `http://drupal.org/project/views` |
| Taxonomy Menu | 6.x-1.02 | `http://drupal.org/project/taxonomy_menu` |
| TinyMCE | 6.x-1.1 | `http://drupal.org/project/tinymce` |

## CHAPTER 7

|  | VERSION | PROJECT PAGE |
|---|---|---|
| **THEME** | | |
| Superclean | 6.x-1.2 | `http://drupal.org/project/superclean` |
| **CONTRIBUTED MODULES** | | |
| Ubercart | 6.x-2.0-Beta5 | `http://ubercart.org` |
| Token | 6.x-1.11 | `http://drupal.org/project/token` |
| CCK | 6.x-2.4 | `http://drupal.org/project/cck` |
| Image | 6.x-1.0 | `http://drupal.org/project/image` |
| Imagefield | 6.x-3.1 | `http://drupal.org/project/imagefield` |
| Imagecache | 6.x-2.0 | `http://drupal.org/project/imagecache` |
| Thickbox | 6.x-1.4 | `http://drupal.org/project/thickbox` |

## CHAPTER 8

|  | VERSION | PROJECT PAGE |
|---|---|---|
| **THEME** | | |
| Zen Classic | Core | |
| **CONTRIBUTED MODULES** | | |
| Image | 6.x-1.0 | `http://drupal.org/project/image` |
| IMCE | 6.x-1.2 | `http://drupal.org/project/imce` |
| Panels | 6.x-2.0 | `http://drupal.org/project/panels` |
| Taxonomy Menu | 6.x-1.02 | `http://drupal.org/project/taxonomy_menu` |

## CHAPTER 9

|  | VERSION | PROJECT PAGE |
|---|---|---|
| **THEME** | | |
| Magazeen | 6.x-1.3 | http://drupal.org/project/magazeen |
| **CONTRIBUTED MODULES** | | |
| Image | 6.x-1.0 | http://drupal.org/project/image |
| Taxonomy Menu | 6.x-1.02 | http://drupal.org/project/taxonomy_menu |
| Fivestar | 6.x-1.14 | http://drupal.org/project/fivestar |

## CHAPTER 10

|  | VERSION | PROJECT PAGE |
|---|---|---|
| **THEME** | | |
| Four Seasons | 6.x-2.x | http://drupal.org/project/fourseasons |
| **CONTRIBUTED MODULES** | | |
| Image | 6.x-1.0 | http://drupal.org/project/image |
| Availability | 6.x-1.x-dev | http://drupal.org/project/availability |
| Fivestar | 6.x-1.14 | http://drupal.org/project/fivestar |
| SimpleViews | 6.x-1.0 | http://drupal.org/project/simpleviews |
| Views | 6.x-2.6 | http://drupal.org/project/views |
| Poormanscron | 6.x-1.0 | http://drupal.org/project/poormanscron |

## CHAPTER 11

|  | VERSION | PROJECT PAGE |
|---|---|---|
| **THEME** | | |
| Fervens | 6.x-1.0 | `http://drupal.org/project/fervens` |
| **CONTRIBUTED MODULES** | | |
| GMap | 6.x-1.1-rc1 | `http://drupal.org/project/gmap` |
| Location | 6.x-3.0 | `http://drupal.org/project/location` |
| CCK | 6.x-2.4 | `http://drupal.org/project/cck` |
| Image | 6.x-1.0 | `http://drupal.org/project/image` |

## CHAPTER 12

|  | VERSION | PROJECT PAGE |
|---|---|---|
| **THEME** | | |
| Strange Little Town | 6.x-1-0 | `http://drupal.org/project/strange_little_town` |
| **CONTRIBUTED MODULES** | | |
| Poormanscron | 6.x-1.0 | `http://drupal.org/project/poormanscron` |

# Index

# C

project, URL 238

# O

**OG module**
6.x-1.3, version 239
project, URL 239
**OG module, community site 104**
**optimization techniques, Drupal**
about 234
Advanced cache module 235
Boost module 235
Throttle module 235
**organic groups, community site**
configuring 104
group, creating 106
new Group content type, creating 104

# P

**page cache**
aggressive cache mode 233
enabling 233
minimum cache lifetime 233
normal cache mode 233
page compression 233
**page compression, page cache 233**
**panels module**
6.x-2.0, version 239
project, URL 239
**panels module, directory site**
used, for creating front page 156-158
**panels module, newspaper site**
used, for creating front page 125, 127
**payment settings, e-commerce site 134**
**PayPal**
enabling 132
**permissions, directory site**
setting 158
**permissions, personal site 22**
**personal site**
About Me page, creating 16
AD The Morning After theme used 8
blogs, creating 17
building, tasks 8
contact form, creating 18, 19
content, displaying 20

content, managing 9
modules 9
permissions 22
publication, creating 18
theming 23
**photo sharing site**
building 161, 162
Fivestar module 164
image submission form 171, 172
modules 163
theme 162
**polls, community site**
configuring 101, 102
**Poormanscron module**
6.x-1.0, version 241
project, URL 241
**Poormanscron module, directory site 158**
**Poormanscron module, news aggregating site**
configuring 211
**posting, directory site**
creating 153
**product, e-commerce site**
adding, to store 136-138
cart, checking out 140
cart, updating 139
Dridget, selecting 139
shipping cost, calculating 140
**products displaying, e-commerce site**
about 141
front page, creating 142
**publication, personal site**
creating 18
**Pushbutton theme**
core, version 238

# Q

**quick menus**
creating, Taxonomy Menu module used 20

# R

**Really Simple Syndication feeds.** *See* **RSS feeds**
**recent comments, Google map site 206**
**remote server**
Drupal, installing on 226

## Packt Open Source Project Royalties

When we sell a book written on an Open Source project, we pay a royalty directly to that project. Therefore by purchasing Drupal 6 Site Blueprints, Packt will have given some of the money received to the Drupal project.

In the long term, we see ourselves and you—customers and readers of our books—as part of the Open Source ecosystem, providing sustainable revenue for the projects we publish on. Our aim at Packt is to establish publishing royalties as an essential part of the service and support a business model that sustains Open Source.

If you're working with an Open Source project that you would like us to publish on, and subsequently pay royalties to, please get in touch with us.

## Writing for Packt

We welcome all inquiries from people who are interested in authoring. Book proposals should be sent to author@packtpub.com. If your book idea is still at an early stage and you would like to discuss it first before writing a formal book proposal, contact us; one of our commissioning editors will get in touch with you.

We're not just looking for published authors; if you have strong technical skills but no writing experience, our experienced editors can help you develop a writing career, or simply get some additional reward for your expertise.

## About Packt Publishing

Packt, pronounced 'packed', published its first book "Mastering phpMyAdmin for Effective MySQL Management" in April 2004 and subsequently continued to specialize in publishing highly focused books on specific technologies and solutions.

Our books and publications share the experiences of your fellow IT professionals in adapting and customizing today's systems, applications, and frameworks. Our solution-based books give you the knowledge and power to customize the software and technologies you're using to get the job done. Packt books are more specific and less general than the IT books you have seen in the past. Our unique business model allows us to bring you more focused information, giving you more of what you need to know, and less of what you don't.

Packt is a modern, yet unique publishing company, which focuses on producing quality, cutting-edge books for communities of developers, administrators, and newbies alike. For more information, please visit our website: www.PacktPub.com.

## Selling Online with Drupal e-Commerce

ISBN: 978-1-847194-06-0          Paperback: 245 pages

Walk through the creation of an online store with Drupal's e-Commerce module

1. Set up a basic Drupal system and plan your shop

2. Set up your shop, and take payments

3. Optimize your site for selling and better reporting

4. Manage and market your site

## Drupal 6 Site Builder Solutions

ISBN: 978-1-847196-40-8          Paperback: 352 pages

Build powerful website features for your business and connect to your customers through blogs, product catalogs, newsletters, and maps

1. Implement the essential features of a business or non-profit website using Drupal

2. Integrate with other "web 2.0" sites such as Google Maps, Digg, Flickr, and YouTube to drive traffic, build a community, and increase your website's effectiveness

3. No website development knowledge required

4. Complete example of a real world site with clear explanation

Please check **www.PacktPub.com** for information on our titles

Lightning Source UK Ltd.
Milton Keynes UK
09 October 2009

144740UK00001B/61/P